MARK

A COMMENTARY

PENTECOSTAL READINGS OF SCRIPTURE

Editors
John Christopher Thomas
Lee Roy Martin

'For Ezra had devoted himself to the study and observance of the Law of the Lord, and to teaching its decrees and Laws in Israel' (Ezra 7.10).

Blessed Lord, who has caused all holy Scriptures to be written for our learning; Grant that we may in such wise hear them, read, mark, learn and inwardly digest them, that by patience and comfort of thy holy Word, we may embrace and ever hold fast the blessed hope of everlasting life, that thou hast given us in our Savior Jesus Christ. Amen.

Book of Common Prayer
The Second Sunday in Advent
The Collect

MARK

A COMMENTARY

ROGER STRONSTAD

CPT

CPT Press
Cleveland, Tennessee

Mark: A Commentary
Pentecostal Readings of Scripture

Published by CPT Press
900 Walker ST NE
Cleveland, TN 37311
USA
email: cptpress@pentecostaltheology.org
website: www.cptpress.com

Library of Congress Control Number: 2018936148

ISBN-13: 978-1-935931-69-0

TABLE OF CONTENTS

PENTECOSTAL READINGS OF SCRIPTURE SERIES PREFACE

The Pentecostal Readings of Scripture Series is conceived of as a forum in which some of Pentecostalism's leading biblical scholars may share their readings of Scripture as they emerge in a variety of global contexts. In order to hear these diverse global voices in one accord, authors are not obligated to follow any prescribed pattern or model of reading, allowing interested parties an opportunity to discern the contours of hermeneutical approaches currently being employed by Pentecostal interpreters. The editors anticipate that by allowing the members of the global Pentecostal community to exercise their individual reading gifts that the nature and shape of Pentecostal hermeneutics will come into clearer focus.

John Christopher Thomas
Lee Roy Martin

ACKNOWLEDGMENTS

I am grateful to Dr. Dave Demchuk and Dr. Wilf Hildebrandt, president and academic dean of Summit Pacific College, respectively, for their encouragement and support for this project. I am also grateful to the board of governors for continuing to give me the honored position of scholar in residence at the college. I have Miss Courtney Gray to thank for transforming my hand-written manuscript into an electronic manuscript. Finally, and above all, I am deeply grateful to my wife, Laurel, for her constant and loving support throughout this whole endeavor.

PREFACE

This commentary has been written to meet the need of the general reader who needs an entry level studies tool to understand the Gospel of Mark better. Therefore, it is written in simple, straightforward language. Further, a knowledge of Greek, though it is to the interpreter's benefit, is not necessary for the use of this commentary. Also, the commentator's hermeneutic for interpreting the biblical text is the tradition of Protestant grammatical-historical principle.

This commentary includes a combination of features that may be distinctive when it is compared with other commentaries. For example, this is a commentary on Mark's Gospel and does not interact with the two synoptic gospels, Matthew and Luke. These gospels were written later than Mark and back and forth comparisons may result in more confusion than knowledge. In addition, this commentary emphasizes the religious culture of intertestamental Judaism rather than the Greco-Roman culture. So, for example, the knowledge of the Pharisaic attitudes toward the sabbath keeping is more important than knowing about Greco-Roman cultic practices. In addition, this commentary adopts Mark's own attitudes about the priority of the Old Testament over the world of people, places, and history of Israel's neighbors.

But Mark's Gospel is not about Judaism or the worlds which surround it. Rather, it is about Jesus and his ministry of redemptive words and works. In succession Jesus revealed himself to be an amazing teacher, a prophet to the nations, Israel's Messiah and the (rejected) King of the Jews. This is the good news which is Mark's legacy for believers around the world in every generation.

INTRODUCTION

1. General Observations

It is a commonplace truth that 'everyone has a story (to tell)'. But this raises the question; does everyone really have a story to tell? In one sense the answer is, 'yes'. But the 'yes' needs to be qualified by the fact that not all stories are of equal interest to a multicultural audience. Nevertheless, the theme that everyone has a story to tell was true in ages past just as it is today, and some of these ancient stories continue to be as important and as transformative as they once were. The so-called Gospel According to Mark is the telling of one such story. It, and the cluster of 'tellings' of the same story by other like-minded story tellers, has been called 'the greatest story ever told'.[1] Fair-minded readers of this commentary will come to agree with this commentator that the epithet about being the greatest story ever told is more than an empty hyperbole.

2. The Setting of Common Era (CE) Judaism

One of Mark's sometime companions, (S)Paul of Tarsus, makes a significant observation about the political, cultural, and world of New Testament times, which is radically different than the earlier world of Old Testament times. In his letter to some young, newly planted churches in Galatia Paul observed:

---

[1] Fulton Oursler, *The Greatest Story Ever Told* (Garden City, NY: Doubleday, 1945).

But when the time had fully come, God sent his Son, born of a woman, born under law, to redeem those under law, that we might receive the full rights of sons (Gal. 4.4).

Clearly, Jesus was born at the 'right' time. Some of the other factors that make Jesus' life and death 'right' include but are not limited to the waxing and waning of cultures.

Close of the Old Testament	Opening of the New Testament
Haggai, Zachariah, Ezra, Nehemiah, Esther, Malachi	Matthew to Revelation
1. The Persian Empire has taken over from the Babylonian Empire and rules the world from India to Egypt (Ezra 1.1, 2)	The Roman Empire controls the Mediterranean world, including Judea after 63 BCE
2. The geographic orientation is still eastward, toward the Orient	The geographic orientation is now westward, toward the Rome and Spain
3. God's people live in two centers: Babylonia and Judea (Ezra 7.6, 7; Neh. 1.1, 2)	God's people are dispersed westward (Acts 1.9, 10)
4. Hebrew, the language of God's people, is being displaced by Aramaic (Neh. 8.8)	The language spoken by many Western Jews is Greek (Jn 19.19, 20)
5. The Temple has been rebuilt and is the focus of religious life (Ezra 6.14-18)	The Temple still stands, but the Synagogue is the center of religious life (Mk 1.21; Lk. 4.15, 16)
6. The priesthood has succeeded the monarchy as Israel's leaders (Ezra 7.1-5, 25)	The priesthood has given way to the scribes and Pharisees in popular religious influence (Mk 1.22; 2.6, 16)

Jesus, a Jew from Galilee, lives in this complex and conflicted society where Herod and his family rule the land. When they displease Rome, procurators such as Pilate, Felix, and Festus rule in their place. In a society where Jews pay taxes to Rome, as well as the

Temple tax, on the one hand, Jews could also be conscripted to aid Roman troops carry their baggage. On the other hand, Jews, including Jesus, had a good relationship with some Roman centurions (Lk. 7.1-10). But the change, which affected Jesus the most, was the de facto authority of the Pharisees, some of whom became his hated and ultimately his murderous enemies.

3. The Identity of Mark

Despite the fact that Mark has authored one of the gospels, he is one of the lessor known disciples among those who are named in the New Testament. For example, Peter and Paul are heroes in the New Testament, but few claim Mark to be his or her hero. The reason for this indifference is not hard to understand. Mark proves himself to be a discreditable deserter. But there are two phases to Mark's ministry and the more mature Mark is reported to be a great helper.

3.1 Mark: The Early Years (Deserter)
In the New Testament, Mark is seen as the deserter, second only to Judas. Luke introduces Mark into his narrative at the time that Herod is murderously persecuting the church in Jerusalem (Acts 12.1-19). After being brought out of prison by an angel of the Lord, Peter goes to the home of a certain Mary, where a group of disciples are fervently praying for him. Mary is the mother of a young man named John. All of the 'Johns' in the early church must have been confusing, so Mary's John is also called Mark (12.12). Mark is Barnabas' cousin and apparently shows much potential for ministry, so some time after this, Barnabas takes him to Antioch where he can be mentored (12.25). Soon, under the leadership of Barnabas, a missionary team is formed. This includes John Mark, though he is not named. But something discreditable happened and after the team arrives at the Port of Perga, Mark leaves the enterprise and sails back to Jerusalem (13.13). As a result, from this time onward, Mark's name is forever tarnished by the desertion, which turned (S)Paul against him. Later, Paul refuses to include him on his team, and Barnabas and Paul have an intense argument about this and these friends, and partners in ministry, go their separate ways (Acts 15.36-41).

3.2 The Latter Years (Helper)

As reported, in several of Paul's letters and also in 1 Peter, Mark matures and becomes known as the 'helper'. Peter identifies Mark to be his 'son' (in the faith [1 Pet. 5.12]) in the same way that Paul called Timothy to be his son (1 Tim. 1.2). At this time, Peter and Mark are in Rome, where Mark is writing down Peter's teachings about Jesus.[2] Paul and Luke are also in Rome, and by this time Paul has an affectionate and respectful view of Mark. Thus, in his closing greetings in his letter to the church in Colossae he writes: 'My fellow prisoner Aristarchus sends you his greetings, as does Mark, the cousin of Barnabas. (You have received instructions about him; if he comes to you, welcome him).' Paul also writes to a certain disciple, Philemon, concluding his letter, thusly, 'Epaphras, my fellow prisoner in Christ Jesus sends you greetings. And so does Mark ... and Luke' (Phlm. 24). Sometime later Paul writes to Timothy, 'only Luke is with me. Get Mark and bring him with you, because he is *helpful* to me in my ministry' (2 Tim. 4.11). And so, the elderly Paul now commends Mark, whom he had earlier repudiated when both were much younger (Acts 15.35-40).

3.3 Mark's Literary Gifts

Mark is a literary genius. The above vignettes are a cautionary tale. Clearly, in retrospect Paul was wrong when he vehemently refused to give Mark, the deserter, both forgiveness and a second chance. One the other hand, Barnabas and Peter were right to continue to mentor him after his grievous failure. Apart from their unreported care of Mark, the gospel that he wrote and which bears his name would never have been written. The larger significance of this is that without Mark, neither Matthew nor Luke would have written their gospels in the shape that they have been written. Therefore, the church's Christology is deeply and forever influenced by what Mark wrote in the decade of the 50s or 60s of the first century, CE.

The apostle Paul made it a truism that every believer is equipped with one or more gifts of the Spirit (1 Cor. 12.7-12; Rom. 12.3-7; Eph. 4.11). It is quite possible that Mark lacked some of the gifts that made Paul such a successful evangelist, but in a special way, Mark was one of the greatest teachers of the apostolic church (Eph. 4.11). This accolade is not an exaggeration. Mark was a liter-

---

[2] Eusebius, *Eccl. Hist.*, 6.14.6-7.

ary genius. The proof of this assessment is that more than 80% of Mark's Gospel forms the core teaching of the gospels written by Matthew and Luke.

3.4 Mark's Pragmatic Beginning

Mark's Gospel had a pragmatic beginning. Early church tradition places the apostle Peter in Rome in the middle decades of the first century CE.[3] As it is to be expected, there he is actively preaching and teaching about Jesus. Soon some persons in his audience realized that it would be beneficial to have his teachings in writing. Therefore, they petitioned Peter to have John Mark put his teachings in writing. The result of this is Mark's Gospel. Eusebius reports this in the following way:

> When Peter had publicly preached the word at Rome, and by the Spirit had proclaimed the Gospel, that those present, who were many exhorted Mark, as one who followed him for a long time and remembered what had been spoken, to make a record of what was said; and he did this, and distributed the Gospel among those that asked him. And that when the matter came to Peter's knowledge he neither strongly forbade it nor urged it forward.[4]

This tradition is significant, for it associated both Peter and Mark with Rome, and of course, because it also gives apostolic authority to someone other than an apostle.[5]

At 16 chapters, Mark's Gospel is the shortest of the gospels. The Gospel of John is 21 chapters; Luke's gospel is 24; and Matthew's gospel is 28 chapters. But these longer, more informative gospels could not displace the genius, which is self-evident in Mark's Gospel and it retains its pride of place among the canonical gospels. Many features of Mark's Gospel reflect his groundbreaking genius. First, the gospel events and preaching were carried out in the Aramaic language of Judaism (note Mk 5.41; 7.34) or Latin, the language of the Roman Empire. But Mark (and possibly some of his predecessors) produced the gospel in the Greek language – thereby making his account truly universal rather than ethnic. Second, Mark reduced the record of Jesus' three years of ministry in Galilee into *one* cohe-

---

[3] Eusebius, *Eccl. Hist.*, 3.1-4.

[4] Eusebius, *Eccl. Hist.*, 6.14.5-7.

[5] Roger Stronstad, *Models for Christian Living: The First Epistle of Peter* (Vancouver: CLM Educational Society, 1983), p. xii.

sive two-part narrative: Jesus' ministry in Galilee (Mark 1–9), and his final Passover week in Jerusalem (Mark 10–16). In spite of being much longer, more informative gospels, Matthew and Luke retain much of Mark's story line. Third, Mark perceived that there were four distinct but overlapping portraits of Jesus in ministry. They are teacher, prophet, messiah and (rejected) king of the Jews. He portrays these functions as progressive self-revelations of Jesus, and identifies each portrait using a 'casting out demons/healing the sick' motif (1.22-31; 5.1-34; 7.24-37; 9.14-28). But these four overlapping portraits carry the weight of an overlapping theme, namely, 'the shadow of the cross' (2.1-21; 3.6; 8.31; 9.31; 10.33). Fourth, in Mark's Gospel these and interlocking secondary themes coalesce into a literary gospel – the 'good news', and from this time to the present day, the four books about Jesus retain the classification of gospel. Thus, with Peter's help, Mark saw Jesus in a way that no one else could see; and by doing this, Mark has given the world good news for everyone to see.

4. The Prototypical Themes of Mark's Gospel

In the prologue to Luke's gospel, he informs Theophilus, his patron, that many gospels have been written earlier than his own. Mark's Gospel may not have been the earliest gospel to have been written, but it is the earliest of the three synoptic gospels, and was known and used by Matthew and Luke when they wrote their own gospels. Mark's Gospel is therefore the key to understanding the gospels according to Matthew and Luke.

Mark identifies his narrative about Jesus to be the 'gospel', that is, to be 'good news' (Mk 1.1), and he identifies Jesus to be the Messiah/the Christ, the Son of God. But the Jesus about whom he writes insists that the characters in Mark's story about him do not speak about him in this way (1.41, etc.). Rather, Jesus consistently refers to himself as, 'the Son of Man' (2.10, etc.). At a time in Israel's history when God's people are becoming increasingly susceptible to Messianic excitement, the self-designation 'Son of Man' is politically neutral and will hide the speaker from the prying ears of the Roman rulers. But it is more. The term is a puzzle or conundrum. It causes people to puzzle out Jesus' identity, and soon they are asking questions like, 'Why does this man speak this way?' and 'who, then, is this, that even the wind and the sea obey Him?' (2.7; 4.41). This term, which is, at one and the same time, both revealing and concealing, is rooted in the Hebrew Bible.

Perhaps the earliest use of the term is found in a psalm of David (Psalm 8). Comparing the glory of God's creation – the heavens – to the smallness of man, David expresses his wonderment: 'What is man ... and the Son of man, that Thou (the LORD) dost care for him?' (8.4). Later in biblical history, the LORD will address the prophet, Ezekiel, as 'Son of man' (Ezek. 2.1, etc.). But the background to Jesus' use of the term as a self-designation most likely echoes the Son of man text in Daniel 7. As one element in a dramatic vision Daniel sees '... with the clouds of heaven, One like a Son of Man was coming. And he came up to the Ancient of Days, and was presented before Him' (Dan. 7.13). This human-like person was given 'dominion ... glory and a kingdom ... which will not pass away ... which will not be destroyed' (7.14). Since these verses are quoted in the New Testament and explicitly applied to Jesus (Rev. 1.6, 10; compare Mk 14.15), there can be no doubt that Dan. 7.13, 14 is both the source of Jesus' Son of Man designation and also his complementary teaching about the Kingdom of God – a subject which dominates his teaching from first to last.

4.1 Mark's Jesus is The Son of God

Against this background Jesus, the Christ, the Son of God (Mk 1.1), regularly identifies himself to be the Danielic 'Son of Man'. For example, early in his ministry, certain scribes charge him with blasphemy for forgiving sins, something which, in their theology, God alone can do (2.7). Jesus defends his action, asserting, 'in order that you may know that the Son of Man has authority on earth to forgive sins'; he said to the paralytic, '... rise, take up your pallet and go home' (2.10, 11). In a later episode, the Pharisees accost Jesus, saying, 'See here, why are they (Jesus' disciples) doing what is not lawful on the Sabbath?' (2.24). Jesus deflects this implied accusation, stating that the Son of Man – and neither the Pharisaic traditions nor the Mosaic covenant – is Lord even of the Sabbath' (2.28). As Jesus' ministry begins to draw to a close, he warns his followers: '... the Son of Man must suffer many things and be rejected by the elders and the chief priests and the scribes, and be killed, and after three days, rise again' (8.31; compare 9.31; 10.33). After Jesus and his three disciples – Peter, James, and John – descend from the so-called Mt. of Transfiguration, he orders them, 'not to relate to any-one what they had seen, until the Son of Man should rise from the dead' (9.9). Concerning his substitutionary Passover death, Jesus teaches, 'for even the Son of Man did not come to be served, but to serve, and to give his life a ransom for man' (10.45). At his trial before the Jewish Council, Jesus prophesies in the words of Daniel that the Son of Man will come, 'riding on the clouds' (13.26; compare Dan. 7.13). Finally, at the Passover, one of his disciples betrays the Son of Man (14.21, 41).

Mark brackets Jesus' ministry by identifying him from first to last to be the Son of God (Mk 1.11; 15.39). But mysteriously, in Mark's narrative, the Son of God is also, first and foremost, the Son of Man, the son of Mary (2.10; 6.3). Enigmatically, though Jesus is fully human, he has God-like authority (2.10, 28), a redemptive substitutionary death (10.45), and God-like mobility (13.26, 14.62). Because his death is redemptive, substitutionary, he is also betrayed, suffers, is killed, rises from the dead and will return to earth riding on the clouds of glory (14.21, 41; 8.31; 9.12, 31; 10.33; 13.26; 14.42). Clearly, in all of human history, Jesus is unique – mysteriously and fully human, yet, at the same time, fully divine. Note that Matthew and Luke, who write later than Mark does, explain the mystery of Jesus' two natures by prefacing their narratives about Jesus with birth-accounts (Mt. 1.18-2.12; Lk. 1.5-2.42).

4.2 Portraits of Self-Revelation

Right from the start of his narrative, Mark demonstrates that Jesus, in comparison to his contemporaries, has a qualitatively superior ministry. For example, Jesus' teaching is superior to that of the scribes and the Pharisees because of its authority (Mk 1.21, 22). Jesus' authority extends to the casting out of demons (1.23-28). He also has the power to heal all kinds of diseases and afflictions (1.29-34). His superiority is also evident in his authority to forgive sins (2.1-12). He (and not Moses) is Lord of the Sabbath. He also controls nature, the wind and the waves (4.35-41). Among the most dramatic of his miracles is that he raises the dead (5.35-42). He also feeds a multitude of five thousand men from a supply of five loaves and two fish (6.30-44).

Apart from some echoes from some Old Testament narratives, such as Moses feeding Israel with manna in the Wilderness (Exodus 16), Jesus' teaching and actions are unique and unprecedented. Not surprisingly, this evokes a variety of responses: amazement (1.22, 27; 2.12, etc.), opposition (2.7; 3.6, 21), and puzzlement (1.27; 2.7, 18, 23). His disciples ask the ultimate question about Jesus' identity: 'Who then is this, that even the wind and the sea obey Him?' (4.41). Mark answers these and other questions about him by giving his readership four portraits of Jesus.

Mark portrays Jesus to be: teacher (Mk 1.21–4.41), prophet (5.1–7.37), Messiah or Christ (8.1–9.50), and, finally, the (rejected) King of the Jews (10.1–16.20). With some overlapping, these portraits are sequential, that is, Jesus began his ministry as a teacher, and though he begins to function as a prophet, he never ceases to function as a teacher. The sequence of these portraits is given on the principle of 'progressive revelation'. The portraits advance from the function that is best known in contemporary Jewish culture – teacher – to that which is least know, namely, Jesus is the King of the Jews. Though these portraits are progressive, each one is introduced by Mark's report that Jesus performs two miracles, namely, 1. Jesus casts out demons, and 2. Jesus heals the sick (e.g. 1.23-28; 1.29-34).

One, Mark portrays Jesus as teacher (Mk 1.21–4.41). This is primarily the role of the synagogue, though the teacher, himself, often trains his disciples on an itinerant or walk-about strategy. Jesus' ministry follows his commissioning by John the Baptist (19.11). The accompanying descent of the dove from heaven signifies that God is empowering Jesus (1.10), and the accompanying voice from heaven signifies that God approves of his son (1.11). As an itinerant teacher, Jesus' ministry begins in the synagogues of Galilee (1.21, 22). It includes functions such as casting out demons and healing the sick (1.23-34). Jesus' teaching ministry also includes forgiving sins (2.1-12). Typical of a first century Jewish Rabbi (teacher), Jesus calls and commissions a group of (young?) men to be his disciples (3.13-19). Finally, Jesus characteristically taught in parables (4.1-31). Though Jesus is recognized to function in some ways like a typical Galilean/rabbi, his disciples slowly begin to understand that he is more than, and greater than a teacher. Having experienced Jesus' control, the wind and the waves, they ask, 'who then is this, that even the wind and the sea obey Him?' (4.41). The partial answer to this question is that Jesus is more than a teacher; he is a prophet.

Two, Mark portrays Jesus as prophet (Mk 5.1–7.37). As Mark's narrative about Jesus advances, Jesus begins to function as a prophet. This advance is signaled by a sequence of three miracles: 1. Jesus casts out the demons, 'Legion', 2. He heals a sick woman (5.1-34), and 3. He raises Jairus' daughter from the dead (5.1-43). The first two miracles are programmatic indicators that Jesus is advancing his self-revelation beyond that of teacher (compare 1.23-34), and the third miracle identifies his new status as prophet. Thus, when Jesus raises Jairus' daughter from the dead, he functions like one of the prophets of old, namely, Elijah, who raised the widow's son from the dead (1 Kgs 17.17-24). Next, in Nazareth, his hometown, Jesus identifies himself to be a rejected prophet like many earlier prophets to Israel (2 Kgs 17.7-25). Following this, Jesus multiplies a boy's lunch, so that this meagre supply feeds a crowd of five thousand hungry men, first as Moses and later as Elijah and Elisha had also done (Exodus 16; 1 Kings 17; 2 Kings 4). Clearly, in ways like his prophetic predecessors, particularly Moses, Elijah, and Elisha, Jesus extends and develops his prophetic ministry to God's people in Galilee and beyond (Lebanon, Syria). But even this progress – from teacher to prophet – is inadequate to reveal the full status of Jesus and his ministry. The third portrait continues to advance and elevate Jesus' own self-revelation.

Three, Mark portrays Jesus to be the Messiah/Christ (Mk 8.1– 9.50). At this point, Bible readers need to remind themselves that the title, 'Messiah/Christ' are the untranslated Hebrew and Greek words, both of which mean 'Anointed One'. In Israel's history, priests, kings, and prophets were anointed to office. Therefore, in Jesus' progressive self-revelation, the one who has revealed himself to be a prophet (Mk 6.1-6), will next reveal himself to be the LORD's 'Anointed One' (Messiah/Christ). As Jesus' ministry advances he has earned the widespread, popular reputation that he is a prophet. Consider the following:

> … people were saying John the Baptist has risen from the dead … But others were saying, he is Elijah. And others were saying, He is a prophet, like one of the prophets of old (6.14). [Jesus questioned his disciples] Who do people say that I am?

and they told Him: 1. John the Baptist, 2. Elijah, and 3. one of the prophets of old (8.27, 28).

But, though Jesus is rightly reputed to be a prophet, he is more than a prophet. In this context, Peter affirms that Jesus is, the Messiah = Christ = Anointed One (8.28). Significantly, Peter's confession that Jesus is the Christ is soon followed by the 'transfiguration' (9.1-8). For the transfiguration to happen, Jesus takes his inner circle of disciples, namely, Peter, James, and John, up on a high mountain (perhaps Mt. Hermon). There, with snow-covered mountain packs behind Him, Jesus is transfigured, that is, metamorphosed. In other words, he radiated divine glory – in contrast to Moses who had reflected divine glory. In this dramatic scene, Elijah and Moses, the two greatest of Jesus' charismatic predecessors, appeared. At the same time a 'cloud' (of his presence) overshadowed them, and God affirmed Jesus to be his Anointed One, his Son. But if Jesus is more than a prophet, what is his anointed function to be? The answer to this implied question is found in Mark's fourth and final portrait. He is the King of the Jews.

Four, Mark portrays Jesus to be the King of the Jews (Mk 10.1–16.25). David is the founder/progenitor of Israel's dynastic kingship (2 Sam. 7.1ff). His kingship is uniquely associated with Jerusalem, the Jebusite city which David and his companions captured (2 Sam. 5.6-10). But initially, Jesus' ministry has been associated with Galilee, where he ministered as teacher, prophet, and anointed one. For Jesus to reveal himself as anointed king, he must necessarily relocate to Jerusalem. Mark reports this relocation in some detail (Mk 10.1–11.11). This is the Passover season, and Jesus journeys from Galilee to Jericho, and on to Jerusalem in company with his disciples and other Jewish pilgrims.

As the actual Passover day approaches, Jesus is arrested and put on trial (Mk 14.61-64). The High Priest challenges Him, asking, 'Are you the Christ, the Son of the Blessed One?' (14.61; compare 8.29). Jesus affirms, 'I am' (14.62). His answer is considered to be 'blasphemy' (14.63, 64) and because of this 'blasphemy', Jesus is sentenced to death (14.64). Mark reports that in addition to being rejected by the Jewish leaders, Jesus is also rejected by the Passover throng. Pilate, the Roman governor, offers to release the 'King of the Jews' (15.9). But the crowd will have none of it. Earlier in the week, Jesus had turned his back on the crowd, and now they turn their back on him (compare 11.11). And so, they insist that Pilate 'crucify' the 'King of the Jews' (15.12, 13).

Mark reports that Jesus' crucifixion mocks his anointed kingship (Mk 15.16-39). The soldiers mock Jesus as King. They dressed him in purple, symbolizing royal status (15.17a). They crown Him, but with a crown of thorns (15.17b). Next, they acclaim Him: 'Hail, King of the Jews' (15.18). Finally, they affix to the cross the charge against Him, which reads, 'The King of the Jews' (15.26). Adding insult to injury, the chief priests mock, 'Let this Christ, the King of Israel, now come down from the cross' (15.32). Ironically, an anonymous Roman Centurion (Cornelius?, Acts 10.1-48) recognizes what the mockers couldn't see, observing, 'Truly this man was a son of (a) God' (15.39).

And so, one fateful Passover festival in Jerusalem, the one who earlier had shown himself to be: 1. teacher, 2. prophet, and 3. anointed one, dies in the royal city as the (rejected) King of the Jews – giving his life as a ransom for many (compare Mk 10.45).

5. The Gospel as Literature

If one were to ask a stranger, 'how many gospels are there,' s/he would get one of two predictable answers. On the one hand, a non-churched person is likely to reply, 'I don't know', and may add, 'I don't care'. On the other hand, most church persons would answer the question, saying, 'There are four gospels'. These answers, both from the unchurched and the churched alike, leave much to be desired, and in this section of the introduction we will tease out a better answer. In terms of the message of these books, there is only one gospel. But in terms of the written record, there are many gospels.

5.1 There are Many Gospels (Voices)

As we have observed earlier in this introduction to Mark's Gospel, the author of Luke-Acts informed Theophilus, his patron, 'Many have undertaken to draw up an account of the things [about Jesus] accomplished among us'. Because of the importance of the Gospel, Luke's observation is not likely to be an exaggeration. But, surprisingly, only two from the 'many' voices have survived. These voices are Mark and Matthew. The others did not survive due to one or a combination of several reasons. Perhaps the most common reason is that in comparison to Mark's Gospel, some of these 'voices' were simply inadequate. Either implicitly or explicitly any gospel would have to meet some standard. The most obvious standard is the one by which the disciples chose a new apostle to replace Judas. The candidate must, 'have been with us the whole time the Lord Jesus went in and out among us, beginning from John's baptism to the time when Jesus was taken up from us' (Acts 1.22). This is the good news, which Peter, himself, preached on the Day of Pentecost (summarized in Acts 2.22-24). Any gospel, which did not meet this standard, would have been rejected. On the other hand, if one may speculate, other gospels would have been rejected because they contained one or more of the twists and turns which characterized the aberrant teaching given by the many false teachers of New Testament times. Examples of this are not hard to find and include teachings such as; a denial that Jesus is the Christ (1 Jn 2.22), the abortive attempt to require Gentile believers to keep the Law (i.e. be circumcised [Acts 15.1]), and living by legalism concerning what you eat or drink in regard to a religious festival (Col. 2.16-23). This kind of aberrant teaching could be found in many churches, and, undoubtedly, some of it crept into some early gospels. But the Christian communities were vigilant, and in the end four gospels met the implicit criteria of 'adequacy' and 'orthodoxy': Mark (and his successors).

As Peter reminded the community of disciples, a gospel is acceptable only if it meets the criterion of adequacy. Luke reports examples of this witness about Jesus. It follows an abbreviated four point witness: 1. the gospel about Jesus begins with the preaching of John the Baptist, 2. Jesus (God's anointed one) had a public, charismatic ministry, 3. nevertheless, the Jews (and Romans) put him to death, and 4. nevertheless, God raised him from the dead (Acts 2.22-24; 10.37-40; 13.23-31). Though four gospels have stood the test of time and survived as Scripture, they are not redundant. Even the three so-called synoptic gospels (i.e. common viewpoint) have distinctive themes.

As every Bible reader soon discovers, no one gospel fully satisfies. S/he knows instinctively that there must be more to Jesus than this gospel. Indeed, all four gospels together leave the readers wishing for more. As John observes: 'Jesus did many other things as well. If every one of them were written down, I suppose that even the whole world would not have room for the books that would be written' (Jn 21.25). Heedless of John's implied closing of these four witnesses to Jesus, many self-appointed persons have, in their own way, written additional gospels. The following chart illustrates the distinctive characteristics of each Gospel.

Gospel	Primary Title of Jesus	Secondary Themes
Mark	Son of Man	Four portraits of Jesus: teacher, prophet, Messiah, King
Matthew	Son of David	Kingdom of Heaven/God
Luke	Son of God	Prophet, Savior
John	Jesus is the I Am	Jesus supersedes the Jewish Feasts: Sabbath, Passover, Tabernacles

5.2 There Are Many *Spurious* Gospels (Voices)

Much of the disciples' oral teaching suffered twists and turns and various distortions. And their written documents suffered similar distortions – additions, forgeries, etc. It became so bad that Paul had to end his letters, which were dictated to scribes, by affixing his name in his own distinctive writing style (Gal. 6.11). Only in this way could he preserve the integrity of his teachings (note 2 Thess. 2.1-4; 1 Cor. 16.21; Eph. 6.22; Col. 4.18, *et al.*). Similarly, the apostle John warned those persons who were tempted to compromise his prophecy of this book, Revelation, and if any one takes words away from this prophecy, God will judge such persons (paraphrase, Rev. 22.18, 19). If the writings of the apostles were vulnerable to being treated in this fashion how much more would the apocryphal writings have been vulnerable. Much of this pseudo-gospel literature can be found in the volume compiled by Edgar Hennecke.[6]

The literature, which I have just written about, is classified as the New Testament Apocrypha. The term, 'Apocrypha', means 'hidden' and therefore 'secret'. This esoteric literature dates from the second to fourth centuries CE. Readers of this literature recognize three motives for writing these books: 1. to give supplementary information about Jesus which is not found in the New Testament; 2. to entertain (i.e. pious fiction, historical novels); 3. to promote hereti-

---

[6] Edgar Hennecke (ed.), *New Testament Apocrypha, Vol. 1: Gospels and Related Writings* (trans. R. McL. Wilson; Philadelphia, PA: Westminster Press, rev. edn, 1990).

cal teaching. It is the third motive, which is of most concern to the church, ancient and modern. This introduction is not the place to examine this apocryphal literature. Suffice it to observe that it was rejected by the church, and, apart from a very few scholars, is still rejected today.

In conclusion, the four canonical gospels – Matthew, Mark, Luke, and John – do everything that the apocryphal gospels aim to achieve, but fail in the attempt. The canonical gospels give their readership a fully adequate picture of Jesus, in the best sense of the word; they are entertaining, and they give their readership spiritual transformation and nurture from the (only) One who is the Way, the Truth, and the Life. This is as true in the twenty-first century as it was in the first century CE.

6. Outline

The following outline of the Gospel According to Mark is intended to help the reader of this commentary better understand Jesus as God's agent as the Way, the Truth, and the Life. The outline may appear complicated, but at its core it is really very simple. Mark's Gospel shows that Jesus ministers in Galilee as a Teacher (1.21–4.41), as a Prophet (5.1–7.37), and as Messiah (8.1–9.50). Mark concludes his narrative by showing that Jesus is the rejected King of the Jews (10.1–16.8). In short, Mark's Gospel exactly follows the pattern for apostolic witness about Jesus. Luke reports that the man who will replace Judas must 'have been with us the whole time the Lord Jesus went in and out among us, beginning from John's baptism to the time when Jesus was taken up from us'. Thus, Mark begins his Gospel with John the Baptist's ministry, reports Jesus going 'in and out', and concludes it with the resurrection.

Title and Prologue (1.1-20)
    Title (1.1)
    Prologue: John and Jesus Inaugurate the Gospel (1.2-20)
        1.1. John Preaches a Baptism of Repentance (1.2-11)
        1.2. Satan Tempts Jesus in the Wilderness (1.12, 13)
        1.3. Jesus Calls and Commissions the First Disciples (1.14-20)
Jesus Ministers in Galilee (1.21–9.50)
    2 Jesus Ministers as a Teacher (1.21–4.45)

MARK 1.1-20

TITLE AND PROLOGUE OF THE GOSPEL OF MARK

TITLE OF MARK'S GOSPEL

The published form of the gospel is, apparently, missing two features. 1. Unlike letters from New Testament times, which identified the author of the letter, which is the first order of business, this narrative about Jesus is an anonymous document. In this regard, this document is like the historical books of the Old Testament, such as Joshua and Judges, which were also written anonymously. Apparently, the story itself, rather than the identity of the author, is its own validation. This contrasts with the prophets and the apostles, whose validation depended upon their calling/commissioning. Even though the title does not identify the author, according to tradition, the author is known to be John Mark, the cousin of Barnabas (Col. 4.10) and Peter's son in the faith (1 Pet. 5.13). 2. Mark's Gospel also, apparently, lacks a title, such as more modern books have. But that is not an accurate perception. In ancient documents from the Near/Middle East, the first line or sentence in the book substitutes for the modern title. Thus, the title of Mark's narrative is, 'The beginning of the gospel of Jesus Christ, the Son of God' (Mk 1.1).

The title to Mark's Gospel contains several key words, which his readership, ancient and modern, need to puzzle out. For example, Mark's narrative is about the 'beginning' of the gospel. This word is ambiguous and may in context have at least two meanings. First 'beginning' may refer to the first paragraphs about the starting point of the gospels. These introductory paragraphs introduce John the Baptist, Jesus, Satan, and Jesus' earlier disciples (Mk 1.2-20). But the word 'beginning' may also refer to the entire narrative, from John's baptism (1.2-8) through to the resurrection of Jesus (16.1-8). In this case the idea is that the gospel, which Peter preached in Rome, had its 'beginning' in the life and ministry of Jesus, which these two events bracket. Many interpreters choose the latter meaning of 'beginning', but there are those who still choose the former, narrower meaning.

The gospel is about one of the many men in Palestine named Jesus. Many readers of Mark's Gospel know that 'Jesus' is the Greek name *Iesous* ('Ιησοῦς), which in turn transliterates the Hebrew name Joshua. Note that the gospel was written in Greek, but the ministry of Jesus was carried out in Hebrew and/or the cognate language, Aramaic. Therefore, in the community where Jesus grew to adulthood, his family and friends called him Joshua, which in its verbal form means 'God saves'. This is an explicit hint that Jesus' ministry will be 'to seek and to save the lost'.

Finally, in the title to his narrative, Mark appends two titles about Jesus. These titles separate Mark's Jesus from all the other Joshua's who lived in Palestine at this time. These two titles are the terms 'Christ' and 'Son of God'. 'Christ' is the Greek word, which means, 'Anointed one'. This Greek word translates the Hebrew word, 'Meshiach' (Messiah, מָשִׁיחַ), which, obviously, also means, 'Anointed one'. In Mark's Gospel and the New Testament, both Christ (Greek) and Messiah (Hebrew) are used to identify that Jesus – like Aaron, David, or Elisha earlier – is God's anointed one. The presence of the word 'Christ' in the title to Mark's narrative anticipates Peter's later confession, 'You [Jesus] are the Christ' (Mk 8.29). Mark does not explain why he uses the ministry to which Jesus has been anointed (priest, king, or prophet) so, therefore it remains open ended for his readership.

The last phrase in Mark's title identifies Jesus to be the anointed 'Son of God'. In the Old Testament, three types of beings are identified as son(s) of God; 1. angels and other heavenly beings (Job 1.6); 2. Israel as a nation (Exod. 4.22; Hos. 11.1); and 3. the King of Israel (2 Sam. 7.14; Ps. 2.7). In Mark's Gospel the designation, 'Son of God' further identifies Jesus as the 'Son of God' by the father (Mk 1.11; 9.7) and a Roman centurion, who witnessed Jesus' crucifixion protested, 'surely this man was the Son of God' (15.39). Both titles – Christ and Son of God – are enigmatic descriptions of the carpenter's son from Nazareth (6.3). It takes subtlety, and also boldness to understand the full significance of these titles, but the patience required to do this will be well rewarded.

PROLOGUE: JOHN AND JESUS INAUGURATE THE GOSPEL (MARK 1.2-20)

Mark does not immediately begin his main narrative. Before doing so he affixes a prologue, by which he populates his narrative with several main characters. In order of introduction, the characters are John the Baptist, Jesus, Satan, and the first four of Jesus' disciples. The last two – Satan and the disciples – are real persons, and they play their part in the narrative, but they also represent others. For example, the presence of Satan represents and anticipates all those who will oppose the redemptive ministry of Jesus. Similarly, the first four disciples represent all those disciples and others who will promote the redemptive ministry of Jesus.

1.1 John Practices a Baptism of Repentance (1.2-11)

The title to Mark's Gospel about Jesus begins in God's eternal decision, which he announces through his prophets. Malachi and Isaiah are two of these, announcing to Israel, 'I will send my messenger ahead of you, who will prepare your way – a voice of one calling in the desert, "Prepare the way before the Lord, make straight paths for him"'. Here Mark combines the prophecies of Malachi (3.2) and Isaiah (40.3) to make a single narrative. This narrative implies that God had a long-range plan, which he has announced beforehand and which he is now beginning to fulfill. Mark's appeal to Malachi and Isaiah anticipates the introduction of the key players in this story, namely: John (Mk 1.4-8), Jesus (1.9-11), and Satan (1.12-13).

Mark introduces John. By New Testament times, Israel had become an intensely religious nation. There was a synagogue in every town and peripatetic teachers were everywhere. But by John's day, this religiosity had been transformed from Habakkuk's, 'the right-eous will live by his faith' (Hab. 2.4) into the work's righteousness of Nehemiah, 'Remember me, Oh my God for good, according to all that I have done for this people' (Neh. 5.19; see also, 13.14, 22, 31). John came 'preaching the baptism of repentance for the for-giveness of sins' (Mk 1.4). His message of the forgiveness of sins struck a cord in the hearts of many people with the result that 'the whole Judean countryside and all the people of Jerusalem went out to him' (1.5a). Some of Israel's leaders were disturbed by John's message, others were curious, but many more came to John 'con-fessing their sins' with the result that 'they were baptized by him in the Jordan River' (1.5b).

As Mark reports it, John's ministry had two foci. On the one hand, he is the prophet like Elijah (Mal. 4.6). On the other hand, he is also the messenger about whom Malachi also prophesied (3.1). Mark now returns to emphasize that John is the messenger of the Lord (Mk 1.7). At this time, when crowds of sincere sinners, or the merely curious have flocked to John, he begins to compare himself to his still anonymous successor. He may be God's appointed 'mes-senger', the highest honor that a man, even a prophet can have, but his successor is infinitely higher than John. His message to the crowds is that 'his successor is more powerful' than he is, evident in the fact that John is unworthy to tie his successor's sandals (1.7). Furthermore, while John baptizes in water, a symbol of the cleans-ing that comes with repentance, his successor, 'will baptize in the Holy Spirit' (1.8). Interestingly, Mark never explains what being bap-tized in the Spirit means, either here in his prologue, or, for that matter, anywhere else in the Gospel. This is remarkable in the light of Jewish understanding about the Holy Spirit. One of their tradi-tions explains, 'when the last prophets, Haggai, Zachariah, and Mal-achi died, the Holy spirit ceased out of Israel'.[7]

God commissions Jesus. Having reiterated his mission as the messenger, John pulls back the curtain on the anonymous One who will be his successor. Therefore, 'at that time Jesus came [to John at the Jordan] from Nazareth, in Galilee' (1.9a). Meeting up with him, Jesus was baptized by John' (1.9b). This is a puzzling report for

[7] *Tos. Sotah* 13.2, quoted in G.F. Moore, *Judaism in the First Centuries of the Chris-tian Era: The Age of Tannaim* (3 Vols.; Cambridge, MA: Harvard University Press, 1927-1930), I, p. 421.

many of Mark's readers because baptism is about repentance and forgiveness of sins, something that his successor need not do. Two points shed some light on this enigma. First, Jesus is doing this on behalf of others and also as their substitute (see Mk 10.45). Second, as Matthew reports this scene, Jesus insists John baptize him, because, 'it is proper for us to do this to fulfill all righteousness' (Mt. 4.4).

Two signs complete Jesus' baptism. Coming up out of the water of baptism, 'he saw heaven being torn open' (1.10a). It is difficult at this distance in time to imagine what this actually looked like, but its meaning is obvious. The tearing open of the heavens signifies that there is an open space of communication between the heavenly Father God and his terrestrial son. This is confirmed by the first of two signs, namely, 'The Spirit descends upon him like a dove' (1.10.b). This is the moment when Jesus is 'anointed' by God, and which both confirms his superior status to John, and, more importantly, which also qualifies him to be the Messiah. And there is still another sign. Now that the heaven has been torn open, 'A voice came from heaven' (i.e. God) saying, 'you are my Son' (1.11). This is an echo of the language which is used in 2 Sam. 7.14; Ps. 2.7 about Israel's David-like King. At this point the Father assures his son, who is now also restoring the Davidic dynasty, 'You are my Son, whom I love; with you I am well pleased' (Isa. 42.1). Mark's description of Jesus' commissioning is bare bones brief, but Jesus' baptismal experience is a pivot point of history. It signifies the new world order, which is irrevocable. Its ramifications still impact the spiritual tone of the world today.

1.2 Satan Tempts Jesus in the Wilderness (1.12, 13)

By nature, many Fathers are proud of their sons. In many cultures, this is especially the case for first-born sons. The question now needing to be answered is whether or not Jesus, as yet unproven, is worthy of his heavenly Father's outspoken pride. At once, i.e. right after Jesus' baptism, 'the Spirit [of God] sent him out into the desert' (1.12). This is to test or prove him to see if he will remain a well-pleasing son, 'He was in the desert forty days' (perhaps an echo of Moses' earlier experience at Mt. Sinai, compare Exod. 24.18). There he was 'tempted by Satan' (1.13a). For such a momentous experience Mark gives no details about Jesus' experience. Mark's only interest – apart from Jesus' being tempted by Satan – is that the desert was a place of danger (from wild animals) and of divine succor; that is, 'angels attended him' (1.13). In other words, in the same way that Peter's mother-in-law fed Jesus and his companions a meal, so the angels supplied Jesus with food. (1.13; compare 1 Kgs 17.2-6).

1.3 Jesus Calls and Commissions His First Disciples (1.14-20)

At this point in his prologue, Mark is about ready to introduce the ministry of Jesus as a teacher (Mk 1.21). When he introduced John into his narrative he gave his readership a summary of his message – 'John came ... preaching a baptism of repentance for the forgiveness of sins' (1.4). Similarly, now that he is about to introduce Jesus into his narrative, Mark also gives his readership a summary of Jesus' teachings (1.14, 15).

In these verses, Mark reports, that having been called and commissioned by God, Jesus is ready to step out into the pages of history. This happened, 'after John was put in prison' (14.a). Mark reports nothing further about John until his martyrdom when Herod had him executed (6.14-29). John's arrest creates a spiritual vacuum in the land, and, therefore, at this time, 'Jesus went into Galilee' (1.14b). Arriving in Galilee he 'proclaimed the good news of God' (1.14c). The good news is that 'the time has come' (1.15a). In other words, God had a long-range plan about 'salvation' and the coming of John and Jesus is the right time for it to be offered to God's people (1.15b). Jesus said, 'the Kingdom of God is near' (1.15c). Now, the precise term, 'Kingdom of God' is not found in the Old Testament.[8] Of course it does not need to be said that God is King over the affairs of humanity by virtue of being creator (Gen. 1.27). Nevertheless, the fact that God is King is explicitly taught in Dan. 2.7. God, the Ancient of Days, gave to the 'Son of Man', authority, glory, and sovereign power (Dan. 7.14a). As a result, 'all peoples, nations and men everywhere worshipped him' (Dan. 7.14b). In fact,

---

[8] G.E. Ladd, *A Theology of the New Testament* (Grand Rapids, MI: Eerdmans, 1974), p. 61.

'his dominion is an everlasting dominion that will not pass away, and his Kingdom is one that will never be destroyed' (7.14c). At different times and in different places, Jesus appropriated from Dan. 7.13, 14, both for his self-designation, 'Son of Man', and the subject of his preaching, 'the Kingdom of God'. In the end, applying Dan. 7.13, 14 to himself cost him his life on the charge of blasphemy (Mk 14.61-65).

Jesus proclaims that 'the Kingdom of God' is near (1.15). In fact, it is as near as Jesus himself, who is God's agent to usher in the Kingdom. Therefore, the issue facing God's people is how they will respond to Jesus and his preaching. Jesus challenges those who hear his message, whether in the synagogue or in the open field, to repent. This call to 'repent' validates and extends John's earlier message about his 'baptism' of repentance for the forgiveness of sins (1.4). Not only are God's people to repent but they are to 'believe the good news' (1.15). Here Jesus urges the uncertain and the skeptical to trust God. Not only is God to be believed and trusted, but also his well-pleasing son is just as trustworthy as God, himself. For those who live under a load of sin and guilt, the offer of forgiveness which John and Jesus proclaimed is good news. Sadly, though many repent and believe the good news, some – especially those who have a vested interest in either the synagogue or the Temple – do not believe and often respond with murderous hatred. But before Mark tells this story, he will close off his prologue by reporting that Jesus calls and commissions some to be his companions and his students (1.16-20).

Having summarized the good news message of forgiveness, Mark abruptly reports that Jesus 'commands' four young men to be his companions and students. These young men live along the northern shore of the Sea of Galilee;[9] and not surprisingly, they are fishermen. They are two pairs of brothers, Simon and his brother Andrew, and James and John, the sons of a certain businessman, Zebedee. Jesus calls them, using the clever pun: 'come, follow me and I will make you fishers of men' (1.17). Jesus is about thirty years old at this time, and these young men, either through their fishing business, or John's baptism preaching, or as part of the

---

[9] The Sea of Galilee is a relatively small lake (7x13 miles) at the northern end of the Great Rift Valley. It is about 650 feet below sea level, and is Israel's primary source of fresh water.

crowds who annually travelled up to Jerusalem at the Passover seasons, may have had previous contact with Jesus. Whether that is the case or not, they left their nets and their boat[10] and followed Jesus.

Having reported that Jesus has called the four fishermen of Galilee to 'fish' 'men' with him, Mark has concluded his prologue. But depending on the level of curiosity, different readers of the gospel may be surprised how much he has not included in his narrative. To illustrate this, observe that he began his narrative, saying nothing about the Jewish nation, their sacred scriptures, or their role in the ongoing history of Israel. Also, Mark is silent about John's priestly heritage, about his childhood experience of the Spirit, or about his relationship to Jesus. Furthermore, he ignores the dramatic events associated with the Christmas Story, such as Mary's 'immaculate conception of Jesus', his birth in his ancestral village, the worship of the shepherds, and, later, of the three Magi. Mark knew all of this information but he seems to be anxious to rush ahead and report the actual spell binding, dangerous, life and death story of Jesus, whom he has already identified as Messiah = Christ and Son of God.

---

[10] A small boat has been retrieved from the Sea of Galilee and may illustrate the kind of boat used by Zebedee and his sons.

MARK 1.21–9.50

JESUS MINISTERS IN GALILEE

JESUS MINISTERS IN GALILEE (MARK 1.21–9.50)

I have earlier asserted that Mark is one of the great literary geniuses of Scripture writing. He takes all of the information about Jesus, which was available to him and carefully decides what to discard or ignore. He then turns what he has kept into a unified, coherent story of Jesus' ministry. But though this story is coherent, at the same time he reports that Jesus reveals himself to Israel through three self-portraits. In succession, through his words and works, Jesus reveals himself to function as a *teacher* (Rabbi, Mk 1.21–4.45), a *prophet* (5.1–7.37), and the *Messiah* (8.1–9.50). These three self-portraits are revealed on the principle of 'progressive revelation'. He begins with what is known (the itinerant synagogue teacher) and progresses through to what is unknown (the Messiah). In other words, each of the portraits reveals a carpenter's son; he is now a teacher; but he is more than a teacher, he is a prophet to Israel, *et cetera*. Following the explicit clues of Jesus' own self-portraits, Mark gives his readers an exponentially developing story.

The words and works, which crowned Jesus' three self-portraits of self-revelation, are finally completed in Jerusalem. The story develops through the final Passover festival, which sees Jesus arrested, put on trial, found guilty, crucified, and resurrected (Mk 10.1–16.8). Here at the end of his redemptive ministry, Jesus is revealed as the (rejected) King of the Jews to those who do not believe, but to those who believe, this man from Nazareth is 'the Son of God' (15.39). But this is not the end of the story. It is the resurrection. 'He has risen! He is not here.' Indeed – the apparent catastrophe (bad event) of the crucifixion is transformed into an unparalleled eucatastrophe of the resurrection (good event). Thus, after Jesus had spoken (to his disciples) 'He was taken up, and he sat at the right hand of God' (16.19).

Jesus Ministers as a Teacher (1.21–4.41)

Having completed writing the Prologue to his Gospel (Mk 1.1-20), Mark immediately begins to paint his portrait of Jesus as a teacher. After Jesus has called Peter and Andrew and James and John to be his disciples, Mark reports, 'they went to Capernaum' (1.21a). This is a fishing village, which was situated about midway along the northern shore of the Sea of Galilee. Peter and Andrew have made their home here after growing up in Bethsaida, another village to the east of Capernaum. The next Sabbath, 'Jesus [and his four companions] went into the synagogue' (1.21b). This 'was his custom when he was at home in Nazareth' (Lk. 4.16). By this time Jesus had proven to be acceptable to the synagogue official and had received an invitation from the head of the synagogue to read the Scriptures and to teach from them. As Jesus taught the people were amazed (1.22). Amazement is a common response to Jesus' ministry (compare 1.27; 6.2; 7.37 *et al.*). The reason for their amazed response is 'because he taught as one who had authority, not as the teachers of the law' (1.22b).

2.1 Jesus Begins to Teach (1.21–3.35)

2.1.1 Jesus Wins Widespread Public Approval (1.21-45)

The authority of the teachers of the law rested on the 'Tradition of the Elders', which was collected and preserved in the Mishnah. When the teachers (scribes and Pharisees) discussed Scripture, these traditions were appealed to. In fact, many pious Jews believed that their authority was equal to that of the Scriptures themselves. And so, the teaching of the tradition rested upon the Scriptures and not in themselves. But it is not so with Jesus, who taught as if he, in himself, has personal authority which is greater than both the traditions and even the Scriptures. Observe how Matthew illustrates this in his Gospel: for example, he teaches, 'You have heard it said to the people long ago, "Do not murder … " but I tell you that anyone who is angry with his brother will be subject to judgment' (Mt. 5.21-22). Further, 'You have heard that it was said, "Do not commit adultery", but I tell you that anyone who looks on a woman lustfully has already committed adultery with her in his heart' (5.27, 28). Many persons in the crowds, who were interested in the truths of God's revelations, were amazed to see it revealed personally in Jesus, and, of course this repeatedly, caused the teachers of the law to be jealous – sometimes to the point of wanting to kill him (Mk 3.6).

2.1.1.1 Jesus Casts Out a Demon (1.21-28)

Just then 'a man in their synagogue who was possessed by an evil spirit cried out' (1.23a). This turned the attention of the crowd away from Jesus – no doubt to the relief of the teachers of the law and their disciples. The man cried out, 'What do you want to do with us Jesus of Nazareth?' (1.23b). Here an implicit recognition that Jesus, on account of his unique authority, can do that which the teachers of the law cannot do (compare Acts 19.14-16). The man continues, 'have you come to destroy us?' (1.24a). Perhaps this is something that the teachers of the law had attempted to do, but failed. The man continues, 'I know who you are – the Holy One of God' (1.24b). Here is the terrible irony: the demon-possessed man discerned the true nature of Jesus' personhood (i.e. the Holy One of God), while the teachers from Jerusalem opined, 'he is possessed by Beelzebub' (3.23). Before this interruption gets out of control, Jesus turns to the man, saying, 'be quiet', and addressing the demon, commands, 'come out of him' (1.26). By this action, Jesus demonstrates that his power is real and not feigned. The synagogue crowd asks rhetorically, 'What is this?' They answer their own question, 'This' is 'a new teaching with authority … he even orders evil spirits, and they obey him' (1.27). Jesus' teaching and exorcism this Sabbath day in Capernaum functioned as a sign to the people of Galilee: 'News about him spread quickly over the whole region' (1.28). This rapid and far-reaching spread of Jesus' reputation is a kind of miracle in itself. This is because rabbinic law limited travel to a 'Sabbath day's journey' (*Pesahim* 9.2). This is less than a mile, and anything further violates the Sabbath work laws.

2.1.1.2 Jesus Heals Many People (1.29-34)

Immediately after the end of the Sabbath service, about the noon hour, Jesus and his companions went to the home of Simon and Andrew (1.29). Incidentally, archaeologists who have excavated at Capernaum believe that they have found the foundation levels of Peter's house to the southeast of the synagogue. At this time Peter reports that his, 'mother-in-law was in bed sick with a fever' (1.30). The reference to Simon's 'mother-in-law', of course means that he is at least eighteen years old, for that is the typical age that males married in New Testament times (*Aboth* 5.21). Hearing this news, 'Jesus went to her and taking her by the hand', healed her (1.31a). As proof of her healing, 'she began to wait on them' (1.31b). Here Mark uses a word, which often translates to 'minister'. This word implies that she prepared a meal for them. Mark has used the same word earlier to report, 'angels attended to him [Jesus]' (1.13).

In Israelite culture, 'day' was measured from evening to evening. This Sabbath day ended at sunset. This is significant because Mark reports that, at evening after sunset, 'the people brought Jesus all of the sick and demon possessed' (1.32). In other words, out of respect for the Sabbath day, they waited until the Sabbath was over and the first day of the week had come. Mark reports two things about this time. One, though the people brought '*all* the sick' (1.32), Jesus only healed *many* (and not *all*). One explanation why everyone was not healed may be unbelief, as would happen in Nazareth (6.1-6). Two, Jesus also drove out many demons (1.33), forbidding them to identify who he was (i.e. the Holy One of God, 1.24). On this day, Jesus is publicly revealing himself to be an authoritative teacher (1.21, 22). It would not be the time to reveal anything else about his personhood until after Peter confesses that Jesus is the Messiah (8.29). Many academics refer to Jesus' demand for privacy as Mark's 'Messianic Secret' (1.43). So, this evening in Capernaum Jesus does the same kind of miracles – casting out demons and healing the sick – as he had done earlier in the synagogue.

Mark uses this pattern – casting out of demons and healing the sick – as a 'sign' or 'marker' at the beginning of each new level of Jesus' self-portrait. The following chart illustrates the progressive functioning of this pattern.

Pattern	Teacher	Prophet to Israel	Prophet to Gentiles	Messiah
Casting Out Demons	1.23-27	5.1-20	7.24-30	9.14-28
Healing the sick	1.29-31	5.25-34	7.31-37	

The above chart identifies the only places where Mark uses this pattern, and it always signifies that he is introducing a new level of Jesus' self-revelation. The so-called 'Messianic Secret' bridges the narrative of the first three self-portraits, at which time it is lifted (1.24–9.9).

2.1.1.3 Jesus Teaches Throughout Galilee (1.35-39)
This inauguration day of Jesus' public ministry is, arguably, one of the most remarkable days of Jesus' life reported by Mark. But though he may not know when or where, he knows that it may be time to move on. To prepare himself for transition, he leaves Capernaum early in the morning under the cover of darkness (Mk 1.35). He is not seeking privacy or escape. Rather it is about prayer. Mark's readership knows what Jesus prayed even though Mark, himself, did not know. Jesus prayed a variant of the following: 'My father in heaven, hallowed be your name, your kingdom come, your will be done in my life as it is in yours' (Mt. 6.9). Jesus' early morning prayer would have been a source of nurture (my Father) and direction (your will be done). So Jesus is spiritually ready for whatever the coming day might bring. At another time Jesus can affirm, 'I have brought you [his Father in heaven] glory on earth by completing the work you gave me to do' (Jn 17.4).

The first thing that the morning brought to Jesus was his quartet of disciples from Capernaum (1.36, 37). But Jesus knows the Father's will for the immediate future. This is to 'go somewhere else – to the nearby villages – so [he] can preach there also' (1.38). Thus, the Father's will is that he travels 'throughout Galilee, preaching in their synagogues and driving out demons'.

2.1.1.4 Jesus Cleanses a Leper (1.40-45)
Mark has reported that Jesus has been travelling from village to village throughout Galilee (1.39). Now, at some unidentified location, Jesus encounters a leper. This man is desperate. His dreaded disease makes him 'unclean' (*Kelim* 1.1), second only to a corpse in uncleanness (*Kelim* 1.4). His incurable condition means that he is excluded from the cities of Israel (*Kelim* 1.1-7). In some way, news that Jesus is a powerful healer and that he is nearby has reached the leper. Therefore, in his desperation he seeks out Jesus, 'and begged him on his knees, "If you are willing you can make me clean"' (1.40). The sorry plight of this man is apparent from his demeanor. This

caused Jesus to be 'filled with compassion' (1.41a). Mark will later use this term to identify Jesus' motivation when he, in turn, feeds the 5,000 and later the 4,000 (6.34; 8.2). In the Jewish tradition, a leper, such as this man is, makes him untouchable. But, Jesus' motivation outweighs his regard for the rules and he 'reached out his hand and touched the man' (1.41a). At the same time he asserted, 'I am willing. Be clean' (1.41b). Mark simply reports, 'Immediately the leprosy left him and he was cured' (1.42).

Contrary to his practice, Mark is silent about other people's responses to the healing. On the one hand, many witnesses might be filled with joy, elation, thanksgiving, and praise to God. On the other hand, strong opposition to Jesus is quickly gathering headway. One result of this latent opposition is that Jesus 'sent him away at once with a strong warning' (1.43). Exercising prudence, he commanded the former leper, 'See that you don't tell this to anyone' (1.44). Nevertheless, he is to go to the priest, bringing appropriate sacrifices with him (Lev. 13.29; 14.1-32) and to have his healing validated.

Jesus' caution about having people talk about his activity has an underlying concern about political and military unrest. This is bound up with Messianic expectations with the Judaism of New Testament times. Political and military ambitions simmered under the apparent calm or peace in Galilee. Jesus knows that reports about his healings will only fire the popular imagination and arouse messianic fervor. This fear was fully justified and surfaced at the time when Jesus fed the 5,000. The crowd gathered, 'because they saw the miraculous signs he had performed on the sick' (Jn 6.2). Added to this, three days later they participated in the miracle of feeding the five thousand. These miracles caused the huge crowd to think upon Jesus as their messiah. As a result, the people began to say to each other, 'surely this is the Prophet [like Moses, Deut. 18.15] who has come into the world' (Jn 6.14). Jesus, who discerns what is in one's heart, knew 'that they intended to come and make him King by force, [so he] withdrew from them' (6.15). In this way, Jesus avoided the kind of situation that caused a certain Theudas and his four hundred followers to be killed or put to flight (Acts 5.36). A similar consequence happened to a certain Judas the Galilean and his followers (5.37). The function of Jesus' Messianic secret was practiced by Jesus in order to protect himself and his companions from being inadvertently entrapped in an episode of messianic fervor.

Unfortunately, rather than doing as Jesus commanded, the leper, 'went out and began to talk freely, spreading the news' (1.45). For Jesus, his miracles sometimes resulted in the kind of 'unintended consequences', which this former leper precipitated. One very significant consequence is that 'Jesus could no longer enter a town freely, but stayed outside in a lonely place'. As an aside, I have often wondered about how many townspeople missed Jesus' miraculous help because the former leper lacked the necessary self-control. Earlier Jesus said to the leper, 'I will' but the leper, de facto, said, 'I won't [keep quiet]'. Therefore, he actually interfered with Jesus' ministry. 'Yet', those who could, 'still came to him from everywhere' (1.45).

2.1.2 Jesus Provokes Opposition (2.1–3.35)

As we move ahead from chapter one to chapter two of Mark, it will be helpful to recapitulate something about what we have learned. For example, we have learned that Mark divides his gospel geographically into two parts: 1. Jesus' ministry in Galilee (Mark 1–9) and 2. his subsequent ministry in Jerusalem (Mark 10–16). We have also learned that Jesus paints four self-portraits to picture his activity as teacher (Mark 1–4), prophet (Mark 5–7), Messiah (Mark 8–9), and (rejected) King of the Jews (Mark 10–16). To this early point in the first portrait (teacher), we have learned that Jesus has amazing authority, power, and compassion (1.21-45). Now the narrative will add other layers of meaning to complement the initial lessons.

Mark often uses a connecting strategy which academics call 'inclusio'. This word has come into the English language in words like, 'include', 'inclusive', *et al.* This technique puts the same word, episode, metaphor, etc., to open and close a block of narrative. For example, Mark reports that the synagogue in Galilee was amazed because demons *obey him* (Jesus, 1.28). He closes the portrait of Jesus as teacher, reporting that Jesus' disciples are afraid of him because the waves of the Sea of Galilee *obey him* (4.41). This phrase 'obey him' informs Mark's readership that from first to last, Jesus has a unique authority which no other person has.

Of course, the Bible reader can only recognize an inclusio retrospectively or from the end. For example, in the episode in Capernaum when Jesus forgives a paralytic man's sins, some teachers of the law have observed Jesus do this and they say to themselves, 'why does this fellow talk like that? He's *blaspheming*' (Mk 2.7). An inclusio is only recognized when the Bible reader comes to Mark's report that at Jesus' so-called trial the high priest concludes, 'You have heard the *blasphemy* … [and] they all condemned him to death' (14.64, 65). This use of the word 'blasphemy' is too significant to be a mere coincidence. It reminds the reader that Jesus ministers under the shadow of the cross from first to last.

2.1.2.1 Jesus forgives Sins (2.1-12)

The theme of the following chapters (Mark 2.1–3.35) is about early opposition to Jesus and to his ministry, not only in Capernaum but also in many of the villages of Galilee. The simmering opposition has a two-fold motive. 1. Jesus' ministry is acclaimed to be superior to that of the teachers of the law (1.28; scribes and Pharisees). Jesus' growing popularity is at the expense of their popularity and quickly arouses their jealousy. 2. The opposition to Jesus also has a religious motive. One attitude of these teachers is summed up in the following slogan: 'Be deliberate in judgment, raise up many disciples, and make a fence around the law' (*Aboth* 1.1 also compare *Aboth* 3.14, 'The tradition is a fence around the Law'). In the judgment of many religious leaders, Jesus, by his disregard of the Tradition of the Elders, seemed to tear down the fence, which they have so successfully built around the law. In the following episodes, Mark shows how this conflict comes to a climax.

Jesus' popularity began in Capernaum, the hometown of his disciples, and it is here that Jesus will establish his home base. Ironically, just as Jesus' popularity began here, so does the opposition that will dog his footprints from first to last. The story line is simple. Having travelled throughout Galilee, Jesus and his companions return to Capernaum. Not unexpectedly, many people gather around him, so that the house is jammed full. But a small group of men have also come – carrying their friend in a sling because he is a paralytic. Filled with faith that Jesus would heal their friend, they dig a hole in the mud roof and lower the man into Jesus' presence. Jesus said to the paralytic, 'Son, your sins are forgiven' (2.5). Even to modern readers this seems to miss meeting the man's obvious need for healing, but it stung the hearts of the teachers of the law who were present. Several of them were probably still smarting ever since Jesus had been acclaimed as having greater authority than they had (1.22), and now Jesus has to add insult to injury.

Jesus could have played it safe and healed the paralytic man in his usual way – perhaps the simple pronouncement, 'Be healed'. But he obviously intended to test these other teachers, so he pronounced the forgiveness of the sins of the paralytic, rather than his healing. Jesus' strategy in this episode provokes explosive tension between himself and other teachers, and they responded silently within their hearts: 'why does this fellow talk like that? He's blaspheming! Who can forgive sins but God alone?' (2.6). As Jesus must have expected, this is to signal the beginning of mortal conflict with these religious leaders. To devout Jews in New Testament times 'blasphemy' was a sin which sometimes deserved the death penalty (*Sanhedrin* 7.5). In one sense their theology was wrong. This is because God's children are to pray, 'Our Father … forgive us our debts, as we have forgiven our debtors' (Mt. 6.12).

In another sense, the theology of the teachers of the law is right. Much earlier in Israel's history, their King, David, learned the lesson that sins, such as adultery and murder, are sins against God, and God alone can forgive their sins. Jesus defuses the hidden conflict, saying, 'Take your mat and go home [walk]'. In this way, Jesus publicly showed that he, the enigmatic 'Son of Man' (see Dan. 7.13) has authority on earth to forgive sins. This authority is validated by the fact that the former paralytic, who had been carried to Jesus, now walked home. This is to the delight of the crowd and, amazed by Jesus' authority, they give glory to God (2.12). The theology of the teachers is right, but, sadly, they didn't recognize the presence of God in their midst.

2.1.2.2 Jesus Fellowships with Sinners (2.13-17)

The first criticism of Jesus in Mark's Gospel is embedded in the *question*, 'Why does this fellow talk like that?' The answer is that 'this fellow' is the 'Son of Man' (2.10). This fellow had earlier been given 'authority, glory, and sovereign power' by the Ancient of Days (Dan. 7.14). The following episode contains another *question of criticism* to be directed against Jesus. The story line is briefly told. One day, as Jesus walked along the shore of the Sea of Galilee, he noticed Levi, a tax collector, whom he invited to 'follow me' (2.14). Later that day, Levi hosted a banquet to honor Jesus. Many tax collectors and sinners, Levi's friends, attended *this dinner* (2.15). The teachers of the law (Pharisees) *question* Jesus' disciples, asking, 'Why does he eat with tax collectors and sinners?' (2.16).

Many Jews in New Testament times believed in vocational sin, as well as moral and/or spiritual sin. One list of vocational sins included the following vocations or activities: a dice-player, a userer, pigeon flyers or traffickers in Seventh Year produce (*Sanhedrin* 3.3), and tax collectors. Those who followed these trades were hated and ostracized, could never become judges, could not give evidence at a trial. More generally, those who followed these trades were deprived of all civil and religious rites.[11] Levi, whom this day Jesus had invited to be a disciple, was such a man as these. And because of this, the question from the religious community arises: 'Why?'

On the one hand, the teachers of the law prided themselves because of their righteousness, but in Jesus' eyes they were self-righteous. On the other hand, they viewed others with contempt, but Jesus treated these despised men with grace and mercy. From the point of view of the teachers of the law, Jesus is both impudent and imprudent. But Jesus has his defense. He quotes a maxim, 'it is not the healthy who need a doctor but the sick' (2.17). Lest the teachers of the law fail to understand this Jesus explains: 'I have not come to call the [self-]righteous, but sinners [like Levi]'. This is why those who did not live by Pharisaic standards gathered around him, because he offered spiritual and moral healing and eschewed self-righteous criticism.

2.1.2.3 Jesus Does Not Fast (2.18-22)
By New Testament times, the practice of 'fasting' has become one of the so-called acts of righteousness, which 'showcased' one's righteousness before men. Jesus is strongly critical about the showcasing of religious piety and actually warned his disciples; 'Be careful not to do your acts of righteousness before men, to be seen by men' (Mt. 6.1). Jesus is not criticizing or forbidding God's people to give charity, pray, or fast, but he opposes the motivation 'to be seen by men'. In fact, Jesus assumes that his disciples will fast and so advises them for 'when you fast ... [do so] that it will not be obvious to men that you are fasting' (6.17, 18). Jesus is so successful at not showcasing his own practice of fasting that he and his disciples ap-

---

[11] Joachim Jeremias, *Jerusalem in the Time of Jesus* (trans. F.H. Cave and C.H. Cave; Minneapolis, MN: Fortress Press, 1975).

pear not to fast. And so, inevitably, some onlookers ask, 'How is it that John's disciples and the disciples of the Pharisees are fasting, but yours are not?'

The practice of fasting in New Testament times is inclusive. If John's disciples, on the one hand, and the disciples of the Pharisees, on the other hand, fast, then Jesus and his disciples should also be seen to be fasting. This question about the failure of Jesus' disciples to be seen is a triumph of Jesus' teaching that they are not to be seen fasting. In this question there is also implicit criticism of Jesus. Disciples did what their teacher did; so if Jesus' disciples do not fast, this is supposed to mean that Jesus, also, does not fast. Both the observation and the question are factually wrong and inappropriate. Nevertheless, Jesus answers their question.

As a result of this question, Jesus uses the question about fasting as an opportunity for teaching. Lesson one is about what is appropriate versus what is only ritual. For example, at a wedding, the friends of the bridegroom 'cannot fast so long as they have him with them' (Mk 2.19). A wedding is a time for festive joy not for fasting. So, it is not appropriate to fast while the groom is still with them. Lesson two compares two examples of appropriateness – unshrunk cloth is not used to patch an old piece of cloth. Similarly, no one pours new wine into old wineskins (2.22). Implicit in this teaching is that one cannot mix the new (cloth, wine), which represents Jesus' ministry, with the old customs (old cloth, old wineskins). The new age requires new attitudes, allegiances, and practices.

2.1.2.4 Jesus Violates the Sabbath (2.23–3.6)
The time when Jesus ministered in Galilee is growing old and it will soon be replaced by a new, better way (Heb. 8.13). Jesus personifies the new cloth and the new wine in the two parables about fasting, which he has just told (2.19-22). Jesus represents new attitudes, allegiances, and practices. Jesus' conflict with the teachers of the law illustrate a clash of wills over matters such as forgiveness of sins, table fellowship with sinners, and fasting as a meritorious ritual (2.1-22). As Mark's narrative advances, these clashes of wills about righteous living will include Sabbath keeping (2.23–3.6).

The 'Sabbath' day is the most ancient of sacred days because it is celebrated by God when he finished creating the heavens and the earth (Gen. 2.1-3). Much later this holy day is written into the cove-

nant of Israel's nationhood at Mt. Sinai (Exod. 20.8-11). A generation later, when Israel is about to enter Canaan, the Promised Land,
the Sabbath covenant takes on a special nuance of freedom from
slavery (Deut. 5.12-15). But as the generations pass, Sabbath keeping is better known for being neglected than for being kept. But
toward the end of Old Testament times, Nehemiah restores the
sanctity of the Sabbath day by stopping all merchandising in Jerusalem on this day. However, and very sadly, he prays to God as if his
action of Sabbath keeping was meritorious. By New Testament
times the Pharisees had also gone down the path of Sabbath keeping as a meritorious activity. This attitude is encoded in the Tradition of the Elders (*Shabbath* 1.2–24.5).

Against this background Jesus' attitude and conduct concerning
Sabbath keeping is played out in a life and death clash of wills between the teachers of the law and himself. Among other things,
Mark reports that spies accompany Jesus to the synagogue, 'looking
for a reason to accuse him, so they watch closely to see if he would
heal on the Sabbath' (Mk 3.2). One or more of these spies is apparently with Jesus as he and his disciples 'walk through a field on the
Sabbath'. As they were walking along, 'they began to pick some
heads of grain' (2.23). 'Look', the Pharisees said to him, 'Why are
they doing what is unlawful on the Sabbath?' (2.24). It is interesting
to compare this with a code for prohibited Sabbath work.

> He is culpable that ploughs ought so ever, or that weeds or cuts
> off dead leaves or prunes … [He is culpable] that gathers any
> wood so ever … and if it is to burn, [he is culpable] that gathers
> enough to cook the smallest egg – [he is culpable] that gathers
> any herbs so ever if it is to set the field in order; and if it is for
> cattle, [he is culpable] that gathers enough to fill a kid's mouth
> (*Shabbath* 12.2).

While this regulation is not identical to the action of the disciples, it
illustrates the violation of the Pharisaic Sabbath law. What the disciples are doing is like gathering enough food to fill a kid's mouth,
and, by Pharisaic standards, it is unlawful.

Jesus vigorously defends his disciples (and himself) against the
charge that they are breaking the law on an issue that is potentially a
matter of life or death. He uses an argument based on historical
precedent. He challenged his accusers: 'have you not read what Da-

vid did when ... he was hungry' (i.e. don't you Pharisees read the Scriptures)? Jesus implies, 'since you obviously don't know I will tell you. He ate consecrated bread which is lawful only for the priests to ear'; and, importantly for the present situation, 'he also gave some to his companions' (2.26). Jesus then reminds his accusers, 'the Sabbath was made for man' (i.e. it is the servant of 'man'). There-fore, the Son of Man is Lord of the Sabbath. In other words, Jesus, and not the law determines what is lawful Sabbath keeping, and what is not. In fact he, the Son of Man, has the same authority over the Sabbath as he has over the forgiveness of sins (2.5, 6).

The issue about what is lawful conduct on the Sabbath day or not plays out in the episode, which follows (Mk 3.1-6). The setting for this episode is radically different from the grain field, which pre-cedes it. This new episode takes place in an unidentified synagogue, rather than in a grain field. However, both episodes are connected like conjoined twins by the issue of lawful activity on the Sabbath (3.1). In the synagogue this Sabbath morning are both a man with a withered hand, and also one or more spies, who are carefully watch-ing to see what he will do (3.1, 2). There is apparently nothing in this situation to prevent Jesus from healing this man on the first day of the week, rather than doing it on this seventh day. But Jesus de-liberately provokes a life and death confrontation. Breaking the Sabbath law is, to the pious Pharisee, a sin deserving of death. The Mishnah explains: 'He that profanes the Sabbath is liable, after warning, to death by stoning' (*Sanhedrin* 7.8). Would Jesus heal this man on the Sabbath? If he does then he will expose himself to the obligatory warning and the possibility of the death penalty. On this day, Jesus brings the matter to a head. He said to the man, 'stand up in front of everyone' (3.3). Jesus then challenges the crowd, 'which is lawful on the Sabbath, to do good or evil?' (3.4). He then tells the man, 'stretch out your hand ... and his hand was completely re-stored' (vv. 3-5).

By healing this man, Jesus publicly demonstrated that it is lawful to do good (a healing). What does the synagogue crowd think about what they have just witnessed? So Jesus asks them, 'which is lawful on the Sabbath ... to do good or to do evil, to save a life or to kill?' (3.4). They have all been taught the following.

> On the Sabbath they may not straighten a deformed child's body or set a broken limb. If a man's hand or foot is dislocated, he

may not pour cold water over it, but he may wash it after his usual fashion, and if he is healed, he is healed (*Shabbath* 22.6; note also *Sanhedrin* 7.4).

This synagogue crowd has stubborn hearts, and would not answer Jesus, because they continued to believe that it was wrong for him to heal on the Sabbath. And in righteous anger, at the expense of his own danger, he healed the man. Common causes often make strange bedfellows. In New Testament times, the Pharisees and the Herodians were mutual enemies. But this Sabbath day, on which Jesus did a good deed, 'the Pharisees did an evil deed'. Mark reports without comment, 'the Pharisees went out and began to plot with the Herodians how they might kill him' (3.6).

This conflict, which Jesus has provoked, intimates to Mark's readers that further conflict will follow. Indeed, it does – all the way to Jerusalem. There his enemies will try to trap him to say something that would bring about his downfall and/or (preferably) his death. But in Jerusalem as well as earlier in Galilee, Jesus effectively out-maneuvers his enemies. The following chart illustrates the pattern of conflict, which was initiated in Galilee (2.1–3.6) and repeated in Jerusalem (11.27–12.37).

Mark 2.1–3.6   Mark 11.27–12.40

	Questions of Conflict	Questions of Entrapment
1.	Who can forgive sins but God alone? (2.7)	By what authority are you doing these things (11.28)
2.	Why does he (Jesus) eat with tax collectors and sinners? (2.18)	Is it right to pay taxes to Caesar or not? (12.23)
3.	How is it that John's disciples are fasting but yours are not? (2.18)	At the resurrection whose wife will she be? (12.23)
4.	Why are they (disciples) doing what is unlawful on the Sabbath? (2.24)	Of all the commandments, which is the most important?
	Jesus' Unanswerable Conundrum	Jesus' Unanswerable Conundrum
5.	Which is lawful on the Sabbath: to do good or to do evil, to save or to kill? (3.4)	How is it that the teachers … say that the Christ is the Son of David? (12.35)

Mark concludes: The large crowds listened to him with delight.

2.1.2.5 Jesus Heals Many People (3.7-12)

At the end of his report about the conflict about Sabbath keeping, Mark leaves his readers in suspense about the negotiations between the Pharisees and the Herodians (Mk 3.6). Some may wonder about who will kill him? Where will they kill him, Galilee or Jerusalem? When will they kill him? Will they use false witness to testify against him? Mark leaves these *questions* unanswered, since he knows that Jesus will not be put to death for, perhaps, another two years or more. In contrast to his conflict with the teachers of the law and other special interest groups, Jesus enjoys his growing popularity.

Mark abruptly reports that Jesus leaves the synagogue and shifts the base of his ministry to the Sea of Galilee (Mk 3.7). A large crowd from Galilee followed him. Indeed, because of the reports about what was happening, 'many people came to him from Judea, Jerusalem, Idumea, and the regions across the Jordan and around Tyre and Sidon' (3.8). The press of the large crowd forced Jesus to minister from a boat, which the disciples had launched. At this time Jesus healed many, and others pressed about him to touch him and also be healed (3.10). As happened earlier in the synagogue in Capernaum (1.23-27), 'the evil spirit … cried out, "You are the Son of God"' (3.12). Here, as well as earlier, Jesus 'gave orders not to tell who he was' (3.12). And so, among the common people Jesus' ministry flourished. This anticipates the crowds of five thousand and four thousand, which later followed him (6.30-44; 8.1-13).

2.1.2.6 Jesus Appoints Twelve Apostles (3.13-19)

To this point in his narrative, Mark has reported both sides of Jesus' reception by others: 1. disapproval and opposition (Mark 2.1–3.6), and 2. ready acceptance and approval (3.7-12). After this Jesus will now 'call to him those he wanted, and they came to him' (3.13). Out of a large number of disciples, Jesus appointed twelve – 'designating them apostles' (3.14). The term 'disciple' means student or pupil; the term 'apostle', which is an untranslated term, means 'sent out' (3.14b). Jesus calls these disciples apostles 'that they might be with him and that he might send them out' (3.14b). Having been with Jesus, they will do the same kind things as he did – 'preach and have authority to drive out demons' (3.15; compare 1.14, 15; 1.23-27). From this point on, Jesus will continue to have many disciples (including twelve apostles); but, inside Mark's narrative, he will never have more than twelve apostles. These twelve disciples – apostles, now have a more permanent relationship with Jesus (3.13–16.8). From now on Mark's readership will have to distinguish between the terms, which he uses: a 'crowd' has a loose relationship with Jesus; 'disciples' are those who have a more regular relationship, but which is not permanent; and 'apostles', the twelve who have a permanent relationship with Jesus. This is a challenge for Mark's readership because he is very reticent to identify the apostles by name; however, remember that as John Mark, son of Mary (Acts 12.12) and (spiritual) son of Peter (1 Pet. 5.13), he would have known all the apostles and/or their exploits.

Despite Mark's striking reticence to name the apostles, here and only here does he name the twelve: Simon (to whom he gave the name Peter); James son of Zebedee and his brother John (to them he gave the name Boanerges, which means sons of Thunder); Andrew, Philip, Bartholomew, Matthew, Thomas, James son of Alphaeus, Thaddeus, Simon the Zealot, and Judas Iscariot, who betrayed him (3.16-19). The first three apostles, namely, Peter, James, and John formed a special inner circle around Jesus. He took these three with him on several occasions including the raising of Jairus' daughter from the dead (5.37) and climbing the Mt. of Transfiguration (9.2-13). Peter and Andrew, James and John, and Matthew and James son of Alphaeus are pairs of brothers. Peter and Philip formerly lived in Bethsaida, three to four miles east of Capernaum. There is one explanation for the reason why Mark preserves the anonymity of the apostles – it is to protect them from aggressive pursuit by unbelieving Jews and by their Roman overlords. Even so, both James and Peter were martyred (Acts 12.1, 2).[12]

Though Mark is very stingy about naming the twelve, when he introduces the term 'apostles', it often means most or all of the twelve. Thus, immediately after Mark has reported the calling of the twelve disciples – apostles – he reports about Jesus and *his disciples* (i.e. the twelve, 3.20). Soon Mark reports about 'the twelve and others' (4.10). After spending a day teaching the crowd, 'he invited the disciples to cross the Sea of Galilee' (even 'the twelve' is too many for a small fishing boat, 4.35). Later, a woman who had suffered

---

[12] Eusebius, *Eccl. Hist.*, 3.1-4.

from bleeding touched Jesus, seeking healing. The 'disciples' including Peter, James, and John (5.37), and the crowd made it impossible to identify her (5.21). After this, Jesus went to Nazareth, accompanied by his disciples (the apostles, 6.7). After the execution of John the Baptist, the apostles, who are the twelve of 6.7, reported to Jesus about their ministry experience (6.30). And so, Mark's narrative proceeds, alluding to the twelve apostles by various terms but rarely naming them. And so, Mark's formula is that, 'all of the apostles are disciples, but not all disciples are apostles' (cf. 6.30, 35, 45).

2.1.2.7 Jesus Is Opposed by His Family (3.20-35)
Mark advances his narrative by once again reporting about renewed opposition. By doing so this Mark maintains a thematic symmetry throughout his portrait of Jesus as teacher. Borrowing a line from the nineteenth century English novelist Charles Dickens; for Jesus it was, 'the best of times and the worst of times'. First, at the beginning of his ministry Jesus experiences widespread public approval (1.21-45). But, this is immediately followed by ominous hostility (2.1-3.6). Similarly, Mark has reported renewed public approval (3.7-12), which, once again, is followed by episodes of disapproval (3.20-35). In order to emphasize this growing opposition to Jesus and his ministry, Mark has spliced together two independent but complementary episodes. The first episode is about Jesus and his extended and immediate families. The second episode is about opposition to Jesus from Teachers of the Law of Jerusalem.

In Mark's narrative, these two episodes are joined together, but before this they apparently circulated separately/independently as follows: Jesus is opposed by his family (3.20-35), and Jesus is opposed by the Teachers of the Law (3.22-30).

In the chart below, the left column documents Jesus' relationship with his family. Mark does not identify the 'house' where this episode takes place (Mk 3.20). It must be closer to his ancestral homes, Nazareth, than to his new 'home base', Capernaum. This identification is probable, his 'family' lives nearby (3.21). Joseph, Jesus' legal father is not mentioned in Mark's Gospel, therefore, he must be dead. Jesus' 'family' then, must consist of uncles and cousins, 'who want to take charge of him' (3.21). They would have heard disturbing things about Jesus' nuclear family before they arrived on the scene (3.31). Mark identifies Jesus' nuclear family to be Mary, James, Joseph, Judas, and Simon (3.31), all of whom still reside in his hometown of Nazareth (6.1). Messengers squeeze through the crowd and they tell Jesus, 'Your mother and brothers are outside looking for you' (3.32). Jesus then asks, 'Who are my mother and brother?' (3.33). He answers this rhetorical question in a surprising way, 'Whoever does God's will is my brother and sister and mother?' (3.35). Jesus is not disowning his family; rather, he is enlarging it to make brother and sister and mother into a spiritual family. So, in the same way that Israel was God's son (Exod. 4.22), so Jesus' disciples are the new, spiritual sons of God.

Renewed Opposition to Jesus

Jesus and His Family (3.20-35)	Jesus and the Teachers of the Law (3.22-30)
3.20, 21: 'Then Jesus entered a house; again a crowd gathered, so that he and his disciples were not even able to eat. When his family heard about this, they went to take charge of him, for they said, "He is out of his mind"' 3.31-35: 'Then Jesus' mother and brothers arrived ... Whoever does God's will is my brother and sister and mother'.	3.22-30: 'And the teachers of the law who came down from Jerusalem said, "He is possessed by Beelzebub ..." So Jesus called them and spoke to them in parables, "how can Satan drive out Satan?" ... I tell you the truth; all the sins an blasphemies of men will be forgiven. But whoever blasphemes against the Holy Spirit will never be forgiven ..." He said this because they were saying, "He has an evil spirit".'

Mark documents Jesus' relationship to some teachers of the law from Jerusalem in the right hand column (above). Because it is thematically similar to the episode of Jesus and his family (extended, nuclear, and spiritual [3.20-35]), he has spliced this episode (3.20-30) into the earlier episode at 3.21. These teachers accuse Jesus of being, 'possessed by Beelzebul! By the prince of demons he is driving demons out' (3.22). Coming from prestigious teachers from Jerusalem this is a serious charge. It is, of course, false, but it is, as Jesus will show, not only false, but it is also absurd. Speaking in parables, he immediately and aggressively repudiates these accusations. The following quotation illustrates this aggressive refutation. For example, he observes:

if a kingdom is divided against itself, that kingdom cannot stand

if a house is divided against itself, that house cannot stand

if Satan opposes himself, and is divided he cannot stand.

Jesus also warns them against sinning by attributing the work of God to Satan. Such an action is unforgivable in the sense that if anyone refuses to accept salvation through Jesus, it is impossible for them to be saved (3.28-30). In spite of Jesus' teaching and warning, they were saying, 'He has an evil spirit'.

2.1.3 Jesus Teaches the Crowds in Parables (4.1-34)

To this point in his portrait of Jesus as teacher, Mark has twice included examples of Jesus teaching in parables. The first example is when he deals with the issue of 'fasting' (Mk 2.18-21). He uses parables about the joy of the bridegroom, new patches and new wine. These parables have an obvious lesson about timelines (wedding) and not mixing the new with the old. The second time he uses parables is when he refutes some teachers of the law about the source or origin of his miracles. But in spite of its clear meaning the Pharisees, who have ears to hear, do not hear (3.22-30). Mark is now about to conclude his portrait of Jesus as teacher and so he devotes considerable space to Jesus as the teacher of parables (4.1-34).

The gospels report that Jesus frequently used parables when teaching the crowds who followed him. More than sixty parables are included in the gospels. Indeed, parables are so much a characteristic of Jesus' teaching that many Bible readers assume that Jesus invented this method of teaching, but this is not the case. The parable, in all of its variations, is often used by Old Testament prophets. The word 'parable' in our English language Bibles is one of the many untranslated Greek words, such as baptism and Christ. The word 'parable' identifies a type of literature that is used to compare something known to the audience with something unknown to the audience. For example, 'the Kingdom of God' (that which is unknown to the hearer) is like 'a man sowing seed' ... 'a man lighting a lamp', and 'a mustard seed, which grows' (that which is known to the audience). Throughout the early decade of the twentieth century, under the influence of the German scholar Adolf Jülicher, biblical scholars often insisted that the parable could only have one meaning.[13] This insight remains generally true for short parables, but often Jesus used longer parables to teach more than one lesson. Mark has collected four parables, long and short, to illustrate this characteristic of Jesus' teaching.

The setting for Jesus this day is 'the lake' (4.1). Jesus' reputation as a teacher was now so great that on these occasions he sat in a boat, which likely belonged to Zebedee, the father of the two disciples, James and John (compare 1.18-20; 3.9). The people were along the shore at the water's edge. Incidentally, this setting, with Jesus sitting offshore and the crowd on shore, forms a sort of natural amphitheater, effectively amplifying the sound of Jesus' voice.

2.1.3.1 Jesus Teaches the Parable of the Sower (4.1-20)

Mark's 'setting' places Jesus in a small boat offshore teaching a crowd who are sitting or standing along the shore. 'Listen!' he exclaims. Having gotten their attention, and settled the crowd, he tells them a parable about a farmer sowing (i.e. broadcasting) seed on the four types of soil, which they find on the hill behind them. Inevitably, some seed falls on the hard-packed pathway (Mk 4.3). Some seed taken from the same sack falls on the rocky ground (4.4, 5). Other seed falls upon thorny ground (4.7). Still other seed falls on good ground (4.8). In order to understand the parable properly, it is important to keep in mind that the seed is all of the same quality; it is the ground on which the seed falls that is different. Jesus had begun the parable with the exclamation, 'Listen!' (4.3), and he ends it with a challenge: 'he who has ears to hear, let him hear' (4.9). His teaching is sometimes a puzzle, and it is important that the crowd pays attention (listen!) and obeys.

However, to listen and obey, they must also understand the parable. So afterward, the twelve and others come to Jesus to ask him about the parable. He tells them that it is about the Kingdom of God, i.e. the rule of God. Its meaning is 'secret' – something hidden in the past, but is now being revealed (Mk 4.11). The disciples are those who hear and obey. But the parable keeps its secret from those who do not hear. Therefore, the result and/or purpose of Jesus' parables is to separate the obedient from the disobedient, the Kingdom of God from the others (4.12).

---

[13] Adolf Jülicher, *Die Gleichnisreden Jesu* (Freiburg I.B. Leipzig: J.C.B. Mohr [P. Siebeck], 1899).

Because the parable separates the obedient from the disobedient, it is imperative that the disciples understand it. Therefore, to make sure that there is no confusion, Jesus explains the parable. The following chart identifies the four soils and their reception to the seed, which falls on them (Mk 4.12). But before he does this, Jesus tells them that the seed is the word (4.12), so clearly it is the gospel (4.14; compare 1.14, 15). And people respond to the good news which they hear in different ways.

	Soil		Response
4.4	Seed beside the path	4.15	Unresponsive
4.5	Seed on rocky places	4.16	Superficial; succumbs to persecution
4.7	Seed among thorns	4.18	Overcome by worldly care; pursuit of riches
4.8	Seed on good soil	4.20	Productive soil (30x, 60x, 100x)

Once Jesus has explained the parable its meaning is plain. Among those who hear the proclamation of the Kingdom of God, many do not respond or submit. Nevertheless, those who do respond produce an abundant harvest.

2.1.3.2 The Parable of the Lamp (4.21-25)
The second parable shifts the agricultural focus of the parable of four soils to the domestic issue of the proper use of a lamp. Jesus asks a rhetorical question: 'Do you bring a lamp to put it under a bowl ... or bed?' (4.21). The implicit answer is 'no'. 'Instead,' he continues, 'don't you put it on its stand?' Now the answer is 'yes'. These questions about the appropriate use of a lamp are a further explanation of the mystery of the Kingdom (4.11, 12).[14] The purpose of a lamp, which has been lit, is to disclose what has been hidden and to illuminate what has been concealed (4.22). Here, once again, Jesus challenges his audience: 'if anyone has ears to hear, let

---

[14] See *Shabbath* 16.6-8 for a discussion about lighting lamps.

him hear' (4.23). He also warns his audience to consider carefully what you hear; 'those who hear [obey] will receive a full revelation' (4.25). However, those who have ears to hear, but do not hear (obey) will lose whatever light they have. In other words, choices about participating in the Kingdom of God must be carefully weighed for there are serious choices to be made – about enlightenment or darkness.

2.1.3.3 Parable of the Growing Seed (4.26-29)
Mark's third example of Jesus' parabolic teaching is about the inevitable growth of the Kingdom of God. Consider this observation: a man scatters seed on the ground' (4.26). 'Night and day' – whether the farmer does anything else or not – 'the seed sprouts and grows' (4.27). That is, 'all by itself the soil produces' (4.28). This inevitable growth enables the farmer to harvest the grain (4.29). Therefore, the kingdom of God is like growing seed – inevitable and inexplicable. And, as Mark has earlier reported, it produces an abundant harvest (30x, 60x, or 100x; 4.28, 29).

2.1.3.4 The Parable of the Mustard Seed (4.30-32)
Mark's fourth and final example of Jesus' teaching, by the use of parables, is about a mustard seed (4.30-33). This is, possibly, the best known of Jesus' repertoire of parables. But many people misinterpret it. The Kingdom of God is not like a mustard seed. Rather, it is about the *growth* of such a small seed into such a large plant (4.32). The amazing *growth* from the smallest of garden plants is proven by the fact that 'the bird of the air can perch in the shade' (4.30). Therefore, the kingdom of God, which is proclaimed by Jesus and his disciples, will one day be large. Soon the book of Acts reports this kind of growth – from Jesus and his first four disciples (1.16-20) to the tens of thousands (Acts 21.20).

2.1.3.5 Mark Concludes His Report
Within another half dozen or so verses, Mark will finish his initial portrait of Jesus as a teacher. So here he begins to close off his report, which is a model of being succinct. He reports that Jesus spoke the word to them with many other parables (4.38). Like every insightful teacher, he limited his teaching to what they could understand. He restricted his teachings to the use of parables (4.34). Finally, when he was alone with his disciples, he explained everything

to them. The modern reader can only wish that the four Evangelists had reported more of these gems.

2.1.4 Jesus Calms the Storm (4.35-41)

Jesus has ministered to the crowd throughout the day. This has drained him of his physical and emotional energy. The crowd shows no sign of dispersing, therefore, he said to his disciples, 'Let us go over to the other side' (4.35). A small convoy of boats joined them and they began to sail across the Sea of Galilee (4.36). Soon, 'a furious squall came up'. The storm was so intense that 'the waves broke over the boat, so that it was nearly swamped' (4.37). Several of Jesus' disciples had earlier, before they became 'fishers' of men, been fishermen. But this storm had them sailing and bailing to keep the boat from being swamped. Eventually, one of the disciples realized that Jesus was asleep in the stern of the boat. With a hint of desperate rebuke in his voice they said to him, 'Teacher, do you not care if we drown?' (4.38). These disciples had witnessed his exorcisms and his miracles of healing, which was evidence of his amazing authority. He had helped others, but now, when they needed his help, he slept through the crisis. What aggravated the situation is that it was Jesus' fault – it had been his idea to cross the lake.

Having been awakened, Jesus 'rebuked the wind and said to the waves, "Quiet! Be still!"' Then the wind died down, and it was completely calm (4.39). There had been a hint of rebuke in the voices of those who rebuked him. But not for the last time Jesus explicitly rebuked them, asking, 'Why are you so afraid? Do you still have no faith?' (4.40). They failed the test. They had known him as a teacher with amazing authority (1.22; 4.38). However, in quieting the sea, he is showing his disciples that he is much greater than an amazing teacher. This reality about Jesus' power to calm the storm left them terrified, and 'they asked each other, "who is that? Even the wind and the waves obey him!"' (4.41). Jesus is now ready to develop a new self-portrait. He is a teacher, but it will soon appear that he is also a prophet (5.1–7.37).

Jesus Reveals Himself to be a Prophet (5.1–7.37)

3.1 Jesus is a Prophet to Israel (5.1–7.23)

As Jesus begins his public ministry, he models himself after the role of the teacher (or Rabbi) in Judaism. The crowds immediately accept him as teacher, recognizing, however, that he has a unique and amazing authority. However, as Jesus continues to heal, cast out demons, and teach, his followers begin to realize that while he is an authoritative teacher in Israel, he is much more than a teacher – he is a prophet. Jesus' ministry, first as teacher and then as prophet, is a matter of progressive revelation. That is, Jesus' self-revelation progresses from the role that is common to their experience (namely teacher) to the role that is not common to the experience of his audience. It is from the lesser role to the greater role. These roles – teacher and prophet – are both complementary and supplementary.

3.1.1 Jesus Casts Out Demons (5.1-20)

The first of the three miracles is set 'across to the region of the Gerasenes' (5.1). As they arrive at this location, hitherto unidentified in Mark's narrative, 'a man with an evil spirit came from the tombs to meet him' (5.2). This man lived alone among the tombs and was uncontrollable (5.3). He also proved to be stronger than the chains by which the inhabitants sought to bind him (5.4). But constantly, by night and day he cried out in distress (5.5). As Mark's readers begin to read his introduction to his report, many of them will recall that the first episode in his 'Jesus as teacher' report was about a man with an evil spirit (1.23-27). As the narrative continues to advance, his readers will realize that this is no coincidence.

The story line is somewhat intriguing, but the details do not materially contribute to the significance of the episode (5.6-12). Jesus casts the evil spirit into a larger group of swine, which ran down the bank and drowned in the lake (5.13). This was soon reported to the nearby townspeople with the outcome being that 'the people began to plead with Jesus to leave their region' (5.17). As Jesus was leaving, which is the setting of this event, the man tried to join Jesus' company of disciples, but Jesus insisted that he return to his family and witness about God's mercy to him (5.18-20). Hearing the man witness about his deliverance, many of the people of the region of the

Decapolis were amazed (5.20). Thus, this narrative about the casting out of evil spirits ends in the same way as did Mark's first narrative – amazement (1.28; 5.20). Again, this is no coincidence.

3.1.2 Jesus Heals a Woman (5.25-34)

The first episode in this section is about a man at the extremity of need. This man has an evil spirit and there is no one who can deliver him from his affliction, but Jesus walks into his life and casts out the evil spirit. The episode, which now follows, is about a woman at the extremity of her need. Mark reports that she 'has been subject to bleeding for twelve years' (5.25). This means that she was ritually unclean for all of this time. She had also bankrupted herself by going to many doctors, but rather than being cured, she only got worse (5.26). Then, somehow, she heard that Jesus was passing by (5.27a). Driven by the extremity of her need, she forces herself through the crowd, which is jostling him as they walk along the path, and she reaches out and touches his cloak (5.27b). When she touches his cloak, healing power flows out of Jesus into her body. She has, literally, taken her healing from him.

Mark reports: 'At once Jesus realized that healing power had gone out from him' (5.30). He asked, 'Who touched my clothes?' (5.31b). Reluctantly the woman, trembling with fear, admitted that she was the guilty party, but Jesus assured her, 'Daughter, your faith has healed you'. He then blesses her, 'Go in peace' (5.34). Of course, Jesus was speaking to her in Hebrew or Aramaic, and he uses the common Hebrew word, '*Shalom*', which among other things also means 'wholeness'. And finally, Jesus reassures her that her healing will be permanent (5.34b).

This episode, of course, has special meaning for this woman who in an instant has been transformed from uncleanness to wholesomeness. However, Mark also uses it to signal that at this point he has advanced his narrative from his first portrait of Jesus (as teacher) to his next portrait. The accompanying table shows the pattern of advancing from one portrait to its successor.

Pattern	Teacher	Prophet to Israel	Prophet to Galilee	Messiah
Casts out Demons	1.23-27	5.1-20	7.24-30	9.14-28
Heals the sick	1.29-31	5.25-34	7.31-37	

3.1.3 Jesus Raises Jairus' Daughter from the Dead (5.1-24; 35-42)

Mark's narrative about raising Jairus' daughter from the dead is his third example of a person at the extremity of need. It begins with Jairus, a ruler of a synagogue, seeking Jesus' help. His need is that his daughter is sick with a fever and is dying. He implores Jesus to 'come and put your hands on her, so that she will be healed and live' (5.34). Jesus agrees only to be detoured by the woman who is at the end of her tether (5.24-34). At this point, a messenger brings the sad news to Jairus – 'your daughter is dead' (5.35). Normally death puts an end to one's extremity of need, but Mark's readership, which has walked with Jesus from John the Baptist's introduction (1.3) to the present (5.21-24), knows that Jesus is not limited by what is normal. So Jesus challenges Jairus, 'don't be afraid; just believe' (5.36). Jesus then clears the house of everyone except the girl's parents and his inner circle of disciples: Peter, James, and John. Accompanying her parents into the girl's room (5.35-40), he said to her in Aramaic, *'Talitha Koum'* (translated as 'little girl, I say to you, get up') (5.41). She got up and began walking around (5.42b). Her parents are completely astounded, but Jesus gave them strict orders not to let anybody know about this (5.42; compare 1.45 *et al.*).

These three episodes illustrate that even for those at the end of their tether; Jesus can do what no one else can do. In addition, these three episodes illustrate that the second portrait, which has now been revealed, shows Jesus to be a prophet, for it is Old Testament prophets who raise the dead (e.g. Elijah, 1 Kgs 17.17-24). Now that Jesus has done the work of a prophet he will next identify himself to be a prophet.

3.1.4 Jesus Identifies Himself to be a Prophet (6.1–7.37)

The Hebrew scripture speaks about a future prophet or prophets who will be a leader or leaders in Israel. One of the important texts about this prophet is found in Deuteronomy. Moses announces to the nation of Israel: 'The Lord your God will raise up for you a prophet for you like me from among your own brothers. You must listen to him' (Deut. 18.15). Many generations later the Lord announces through Malachi, the last of the Old Testament prophets, 'See, I will send you the prophet Elijah before the great and terrible day of the Lord comes' (Mal. 4.5). And then the gift of prophecy ceases – for four hundred years! On the one hand, this background helps explain why the common people identified Jesus as a *prophet*. On the other hand, it also explains one reason (but not the only reason) why Jesus was rejected as a *false* prophet.

3.1.4.1 Jesus Ministers in Nazareth (6.1-6)
Much of the ministry of Jesus which Mark has already reported, takes place in and around Capernaum and Bethsaida, but in this narrative Jesus returns to his hometown, Nazareth (Mk 6.1). Implicit in this narrative is the fact that he has taught in the synagogue many times before (for otherwise he would not be teaching there now, 6.1a). But instead of teaching the Sabbath day lesson in the expected traditional way, Jesus teaches a lesson announcing, 'the Kingdom of God is near. Repent and believe the good news' (1.15). And so, as Jesus teaches about this theme many congregants are amazed (6.1b), but there is a hostile undercurrent that will soon erupt. They ask one another, 'Where did this man get these things?' (6.2a). They also add, 'he even does miracles' (6.2). Those who react with consternation apparently remember stories about his mother's irregular pregnancy. While the synagogue crowd knows who Jesus' mother is (Mary), they apparently do not know who his father is. Some of the crowd begin to denigrate him. They know him 'as a carpenter' (6.3), and they ask, 'aren't his brother here?' (James, Joseph, Judas, and Simon, 6.3c). Instead of welcoming the return of Jesus to Nazareth, they not only denigrate him, '[but] they took offense at him' (6.3d).

His townspeople took offense at him; in turn, he took offense at them. He has come home, having done the work of a prophet, but they refuse to honor him as a prophet (6.5). They refuse to acknowledge him as someone who has been called and commissioned a prophet (1.9-11). Therefore, because of their unbelief he could not do many miracles there. In other words, if his miracles are the work of a prophet, and they rejected his claims to prophethood, they have cut themselves off from the blessings which prophethood brings. Mark concludes his narrative, observing an ironic note: at Capernaum, the people are amazed at him (1.22), but at Nazareth, because of their unbelief, he is amazed at his family and friends (6.6).

3.1.4.2 Jesus Sends Out the Twelve (6.7-13)

Jesus' experience at Nazareth was unsuccessful, for rather than welcoming him home, many of his friends and family rejected him. Leaving Nazareth, he 'went around teaching from village to village' (Mk 6.7). Though he, himself, had been rejected, he must have considered that the time was propitious for sending out the Twelve. He bestowed his authority on them, and 'sent them out two by two' (6.7). Having arrived at this point in his ministry – e.g. raising the dead and publicly identifying himself to be a prophet (6.4) – he is now beginning to extend his prophetic ministry. This development is modeled after the two charismatic prophets, Elijah and Elisha and their prophets in training, 'the company of the prophets (e.g. 2 Kgs 2.3, 7, *et al.*). But the Elijah/Elisha narratives give minimal information about these 'prophets-in-training', so Jesus adapts his role as leader to that of teacher and his students.

The rabbinic model included the following guidelines: the disciple was to remember everything faithfully (*Aboth* 3.5). Also, the disciple was never to alter the teaching, which he had received (*Eduyoth* 1.3). The highest praise given to a student was to liken him to be 'a plastered cistern which loses not one drop' (*Aboth* 2.8). If these guidelines for rabbinic students were rigorous, how much more would Jesus have expected from his 'messengers of the prophet'.

These were Jesus' instructions:

They are to take nothing for the journey, except a staff – no bread, no bag, and no money.
They are to wear sandals, but are not to take an extra tunic.
If they are welcomed into a house, they are to stay there until they leave that town.
If they are not welcomed in any place, or listened to, they are to

shake the dusk off their feet when they leave, as a testimony against them (compare Acts 13.51).

These instructions are about the 'deportment' of the disciples and not about the content of their ministry. Without giving any examples of their ministry, Mark reports: 'they preached that people should repent' (6.12). This is an echo of the preaching of both John the Baptist (1.4) and Jesus (1.15). They also cast out many demons and healed many sick people – signs that the Kingdom of God has drawn near (1.15).

3.1.4.3 Jesus is Reputed to be a Prophet (6.14-29)

Mark has just reported about the success of the Twelve as peripatetic (i.e. walk about) prophets-in-training. He now shifts his focus back to Jesus, who by this time has developed the reputation of being a famous prophet. His report has two parts: 1. Jesus' reputation as a prophet (6.14-15) and 2. the martyrdom of John the Baptist, Jesus' prophetic predecessor (6.16-29).

As Jesus' ministry has been advancing, so has his reputation. His various audiences no longer think about him merely as an amazing teacher, they now think of his as a prophet. But his reputation is confused and confusing. Mark introduces this situation from the perspective of King Herod, son of Herod the Great (6.14a). He had been hearing rumors that the prophet who is named Jesus is also, 'John the Baptist [who] has been raised from the dead' (6.14b). As proof for their speculation, they had heard about the miraculous powers which were working in him (6.14b). Others said, 'He is Elijah' (6.15), but still others championed a third option, specifically, 'he is a prophet, like one of the prophets of long ago' (6.15b). Though the people are confused about Jesus' identity – John, Elijah, or another prophet – they are unanimous about one thing: Jesus is a prophet. And he is not just any prophet. Whatever his name, he is a special prophet like either John the Baptist or Elijah.

King Herod is perplexed concerning the rumors and speculations regarding the identity of Jesus, 'John, the man I beheaded, he has been raised from the dead?' (6.16). Herod had earlier married Herodias, Philip the Tetrarch's wife. John had criticized them for this act of adultery, 'so Herodias nursed a grudge against him' (6.19). On one occasion the daughter of Herodias entertained Herod and his guests at a banquet, and Herod capriciously offered her anything which she wanted. Her hate-filled mother told her to ask for John the Baptist's head on a platter. And so, the despicable deed was done. And in this way, the prophet John (and not Stephen [Acts 6.8-7.60]) became the first Christian martyr. John, the first Christian prophet, has been succeeded by Jesus, God's anointed prophet.

3.1.4.4 Jesus Confirms That He Is a Prophet (6.30–7.23)

Mark continues to fill out his portrait of Jesus as prophet. First, when Jesus raised Jairus' daughter from the dead he was doing the work of charismatic prophets, such as Elijah and Elisha (1 Kgs 17.17-24; 2 Kgs 4.28-37). Second, in the synagogue at Nazareth, Jesus claims to be a hometown prophet (Mk 6.4). Third, he sends out the Twelve, as 'messengers of the prophet' (6.7-13). Fourth, his prophetic word and works develop his reputation as a prophet (6.14-16). In the next several episodes, Jesus will continue to confirm that his reputation is fully justified.

Anyone can claim to be a prophet, but often their claim is illusionary or fraudulent. This was as true in New Testament times as it is in contemporary Christendom. But it is not so with Jesus. He validates his works, claims a reputation by multiplying a small supply of bread and fish – five loaves of bread and two fish – into enough bread and fish to feed a crowd of five thousand men (plus women and children) (Mk 6.31-44). The disciples, because of their earlier ministry (6.7-13), are now 'bona fide' messengers of the prophet and return to Jesus, 'reporting to him all they have done and taught' (6.30). But once again, a crowd gathers and they begin to press against Jesus' own disciples (6.30, 31). So Jesus takes his disciples to a quiet place for food and rest (6.31). However, though Jesus and his disciples have crossed the Sea of Galilee by boat, the crowd followed him, walking along the shore (6.32-34). After the crowd catches up to Jesus, who had already arrived by boat, Jesus feels compassion on them because they are like sheep without a shepherd (6.34). It is now late in the day, and Jesus is faced with an opportunity to feed the crowd, but the disciples could only think of the logistical problems, which made it an impossible thing to do – supermarkets and banks had not yet been invented.

This is the setting for Jesus to confirm his prophethood. In this large crowd only five loaves of bread can be found (6.38). Undaunted and after praying, Jesus (continually) breaks the bread and fish into pieces, and the disciples spread out among the crowd to distribute the food (6.39-41). In this way, a crowd of five thousand ate and was satisfied (6.42-44). Significantly, twelve baskets full were left over. So this is a miracle of multiplying food, which confirms Jesus' claims to prophethood. Though the details are different, this miracle is like Moses and the daily supply of manna (i.e. bread from heaven) in the wilderness (Exod. 16.1-36). It is also like the daily supply of food by which the widow of Zarephath fed Elijah (1 Kgs 17.12-16). Jesus' miracle is also like Elisha feeding one hundred men from twenty loaves with some left over (2 Kgs 4.43, 44). His episode of Jesus feeding the five thousand not only shows him to be a prophet, but it specifically illustrates that he is modelling his prophetic ministry after those of the charismatic prophets, namely, Moses, Elijah, and Elisha. But, strangely, the twelve disciples did not understand the message of the twelve baskets of bread and fish which they were holding in their hands.

If feeding the five thousand confirms that Jesus is a charismatic prophet like Moses, Elijah, and Elisha, then walking on water is a second confirmatory miracle. It happens this way: 'Immediately [after feeding] Jesus had his disciples get into the boat and go on ahead of him to Bethsaida' (Mk 6.45). Jesus, himself, finds a quiet spot to pray. As the evening advances, the disciples had made slow progress, 'because the wind was against them' (6.45). In this setting, Jesus went to them, 'walking on the lake' (6.48). Testing their spiritual growth, he made as if to walk by them. Jesus' disciples do not recognize him, but 'they thought he was a ghost' (6.49), because 'they all saw him and were terrified' (6.50). After their recent experience as 'prophets-in-training', this was a dismal failure, and Jesus had to cry out, 'Take courage!' 'It is I!' 'Don't be afraid' (6.50b). This assurance is an echo of Ps. 77.20, where in poetic language the one who speaks ('It is I.') is Yahweh and who walks on the pathway of the sea. Jesus joins his disciples in the boat, and 'the wind died down' (6.51). This is an echo of the earlier episode of Jesus calming the storm (4.35-41). The disciples were completely amazed – but they shouldn't have been (6.52). Mark reports their failure: 'for they had not understood about the loaves, for their hearts were hardened' (6.52). The disciple's lack of growth/understanding becomes one of several secondary themes as Jesus moves ever closer to his forthcoming destiny in Jerusalem.

Much chagrined at their embarrassing failure, the disciples now speedily crossed the lake in silence (if we may speculate). However, the crowd, which had not dispersed, found Jesus and his prophets-in-training at Gennesret (the northeast shoreline of the Sea of Galilee [Mk 6.53]). News of Jesus' arrival quickly spread. and wherever he went, the sick crowded around him to be healed. Those who couldn't walk, 'were placed in the marketplace', so that they could 'touch even the edge of his clock, and all who touched him were healed' (6.56). This anticipates healing by Peter's shadow in Jerusalem (Acts 5.12-16), and healing by Paul's aprons and handkerchiefs in Ephesus (Acts 19.11).

The fourth confirmatory episode is a clash between Jesus and his enemies, some Pharisees and Teachers of the Law. This clash is about the ongoing issue of authority – is it to be found in the Traditions of the Elders or is it to be found in Jesus? This episode arises out of the observation by these critics of Jesus that some of his followers (were eating food 'with hands that were "unclean" that is, unwashed', Mk 7.2). Early church tradition has it that Mark recorded Peter's preaching when the two were in Rome in the sixties CE. If this is correct, it explains why Mark gives an editorial comment, 'the Pharisees and all the Jews do not eat unless they give their hands a ceremonial washing ... And they observe many other traditions' (7.3, 4). On the surface, this seems to be a rather petty issue, but the Pharisees press the issue, asking Jesus, 'Why don't your disciples live according to theTradition of the Elders, instead of eating their food with unclean hands?' (7.4). In this and other ways the Pharisees attempted to emulate the ceremonial purity regulations, which the priests followed when they performed their ceremonial duties at the Temple.

This challenge to Jesus about the need for ceremonial purity is deeper than a surface issue. Once again, it is about the validity of the 'authority of the Elders'. It continues the earlier confrontational episodes where it asked, 'Why does this fellow talk like that?' (i.e. forgives sins). 'He is blaspheming' (Mk 2.7); 'why does he [Jesus] eat with tax-gatherers and sinners?' (2.16); and 'why are they [the disciples] doing what is not lawful?' (2.24). Right from his earliest days of public ministry, Jesus demonstrates a level of authority different than the teacher of the law and their transitions, and this concern about ceremonial purity is another salvo in the conflict between the two parties.

In this clash, Jesus comes out with both guns blazing. For his defense he appeals to Isaiah. By doing this, Jesus insists that he will fight the battle about authority from the Scriptures, and not from the Traditions of the Elders. Therefore, well did Isaiah write, 'These people honor me with their lips, but their hearts are far from me' (Mk 7.6; Isa. 29.13). Using Isaiah as his authority he observes, 'they worship me in vain; their teachings are but rules taught by men' (Isa. 29.13). Based on the Scripture, Jesus accuses his opponents, 'You have let go of the commands of God and are holding onto the traditions of men' (Mk 7.8). Therefore, the Pharisaic traditions, intended as a fence around the law (*Aboth* 1.1) invalidated the law.

Jesus concludes his defense, firing off a final salvo (Mk 7.9-13). It is about the practice of 'corban', which is referred to more than eighty times in the Old Testament. Corban denotes an offering to God. In his commentary on Mark, C.E.B. Canfield explains: 'That which is offered to God becomes holy and so is no longer available for common use'.[15] The law teaches God's people to honor their parents (Exod. 20.12). By designating his resources, therefore, sons who practice this tradition (and others), nullify the word of God. But Corban is simply an example, for 'you [Pharisees] do many other things like that' (7.9-13).

Earlier in his ministry, Jesus had clashed with the Pharisees about the Tradition of the Elders concerning the Sabbath (Mk 2.24-28). At that time, he not only repudiated the authority of the tradition, but he also insisted that he, and not even scripture, had the ultimate authority. Now he has clashed with a group of Pharisees about the authority of the tradition concerning what is clean and what is unclean (7.1-13). Mark reports, 'again Jesus called a crowd to him' (7.14). His purpose is that he can teach them about what is clean and what is unclean. The determining factor is that food which goes into the stomach and is then eliminated does not make a person unclean (7.16).

From this vantage point of a modern reader, Jesus' teaching is clear and definitive, but the disciples, who have been indoctrinated

---

[15] C.E.B. Cranfield, *The Gospel According to Saint Mark* (Cambridge: Cambridge University Press, 1966), pp. 235-38.

in Pharisaic traditions, are uncertain about what Jesus means. Their uncertainty is compounded by the fact that Jesus is here speaking in a parable (Mk 7.17). Speaking to Jesus privately, they ask him what the parable means, only to receive a rebuke for being so dull (7.18). Nevertheless, Jesus explains that food does not defile a person because it goes into his stomach and not into his heart (7.19). At this point, Mark states the definitive principle about 'food' – Jesus has declared all foods to be clean (7.19b). The irony here is that the Pharisees have been chastised by Jesus for nullifying the law by their tradition (7.13), but here Jesus nullified scripture itself by his teaching. Clearly, only 'the Son of Man' has the depth of authority, which it takes to override scripture (Dan. 7.13, 14).

So that the disciples clearly understand, Jesus reiterates, food does not defile a person because it goes into his or her stomach; rather it is that which comes out of the heart of a person, which defiles a person. Finally, Jesus gives a list of examples of typical things which defile a person: 'evil thoughts, sexual immorality, theft, murder, adultery, greed, malice, deceit, lewdness, envy, slander, arrogance, and folly' (Mk 7.21-23). Paul calls his examples of human sinfulness, 'the sinful nature' (Gal. 5.19-21). Someone might protest, 'I sometimes do or think in some of these ways, but it's not sin; it's just my human nature'. Jesus would retort, 'That's right!' Human nature is sinful nature; that is, 'all these evils come from inside and make a man unclean' (7.23).

3.2 Jesus is a Prophet to the Gentiles (7.24-37)

This is the third time that Mark introduces Jesus' ministry by the pattern, 1. he casts out demons and 2. he heals the sick. This time there is one significant variation. This is that Jesus does these things in the lands of the Gentiles (Mk 7.24-37). This facet of Jesus' ministry identifies him to be the prophet to the Gentiles. The two episodes in this section will complete Mark's portrait of Jesus as Prophet, and prepare his readership for the next portrait, 'Jesus is the Messiah' (Mk 8.1–9.50).

In the two episodes under review, Jesus consciously and deliberately goes to Gentile lands – Tyre and Sidon and the Decapolis (Syria) – and to Gentile people. By doing this, he will replicate the ministries of the two charismatic prophets, Elijah and Elisha. Lest this observation regarding Mark's narrative strategies be rejected as arbitrary or fanciful, let us look at Luke's narrative in comparison to Mark's.

Jesus affirms:

> I tell you the truth, no prophet is accepted in his hometown. There were many widows in Israel … Yet Elijah was not sent to any of them, but to a widow in Zarephath in the region of Sidon. And there were many in Israel with leprosy, yet not one of them was cleansed – only Naaman the Syrian (Lk. 4.24-27).

In their own distinctive ways both Mark and Luke show that at this time in his ministry, Jesus is modeling his prophetic ministry after the two charismatic prophets, Elijah and Elisha, who turned their backs on Israel and ministered to strangers.

3.2.1 Jesus Ministers In the Vicinity of Tyre (7.24-30)

After teaching the disciples and the crowd about clean and unclean (Mk 7.14-23), 'Jesus left that place and went to the vicinity of Tyre' (7.24a). This is significant in Jesus' ministry, for Tyre is a city of Gentiles on the borderlands between Lebanon and Israel. His motive is to escape the notice of Jewish crowds, which constantly formed wherever he went (7.24b). Yet he could not keep his presence secret (7.24c). One of those who heard about his presence was 'a woman whose little daughter was possessed by an evil spirit' (7.25). This episode is so unusual that Mark emphasized that 'the woman was a Greek, born in Syrian Phoenicia' (7.26). Coming to Jesus, 'she fell at his feet [and] she begged Jesus to drive the evil spirit out of her daughter' (7.26c). To many of Mark's readers, the dialogue that follows seems totally out of character for Jesus. He says, 'first let the children eat all they want,' adding, 'for it is not right to take the children's bread and toss it to their dogs' (7.27). Her desperation drove her to reply, 'yes, Lord, but even the dogs under the table eat the children's crumbs' (7.28). In their short dialogue, the 'children' are the 'children of Israel', and the 'dogs' are the 'Gentiles', such as this woman; however, it seems to Mark's readership that Jesus' reply has been a test, and it meets with Jesus' approval. He tells her, 'for such a reply you may go; the demon has left your daughter' (7.29). Having completed her mission, she returns home to find her daughter lying on her bed, the demon gone (7.30).

3.2.2 Jesus Ministers in the Region of the Decapolis (7.31-37)

The experience of Jesus in the vicinity of Tyre (7.24-30) is close to being the final brush strokes in his self-portrait as prophet. Only one last brush stroke is needed. In order to complete his ministry as prophet like Elisha, he must now heal a Gentile. To paint this final stroke, 'Jesus left the vicinity of Tyre [the location Elijah's ministry to a Gentile widow], and went through Sidon, down to the Sea of Galilee and into the region of Decapolis' (7.31). So, to complete this portrait, Elisha-like brush strokes, he has had to traverse upper Galilee from the Mediterranean, past the Sea of Galilee and across the Jordan river to the east bank (Syria). Arriving at his geographical destination, 'some people brought to him a man who was deaf and could hardly talk' (7.32a). These family and/or friends 'begged him [i.e. Jesus] to place his hand upon the man' (7.32b). Somehow they have heard that for those who need it, Jesus' touch is a healing touch.

Jesus takes the man away from the distractions of the crowd. Then, 'he put his fingers into the man's ears' (7.33a) – to communicate to this deaf man that he will be healed of his deafness. Next, 'he touched the man's tongue' (7.33b) – an appropriate sign that he will heal the man's speech, but Jesus' healing power is not to be found in his touch. Rather, it is to be found in his words. He commands, '*Ephphatha*' which means, 'be opened' (7.34). As a result of this command, the man was completely healed – both his ears and his tongue.

Jesus can command ears and closed mouths to be 'opened', and the physical body obeys him, but from as far back as Mark 1, Jesus can command those who have been healed by him to be quiet about their healing, only to be repeatedly disobeyed. And such is also the situation here in Decapolis. People are 'overwhelmed with amazement' and the more Jesus asked for quiet, the more they talked about it (7.36). As happened so often, the crowd brought the man to Jesus to be healed, and when he is healed they are overwhelmed that he did the very thing they asked him to do (7.37).

In his second self-portrait, Jesus becomes the charismatic prophet and his companions will become the charismatic prophets-in-training (Mk 7.7-13). Initially, Jesus proved to be an amazing teacher with unpreceded authority, but by this next step forward he portrays himself to be an amazing prophet. For example, he raises the dead.

He also multiplies a little food into much food. He walks on water, and like Elijah and Elisha, he ministers to Gentiles. This is amazing, but it doesn't match his next self-portrait, which will climax his ministry in Galilee. Jesus' third self-portrait is that he is the Messiah.

Jesus is the Messiah (8.1–9.50)

Jesus began his ministry throughout Galilee by revealing himself to be a teacher. The role of teacher was associated with the synagogue and it was the ready-made place to begin his ministry. But once he had fully established himself as a teacher, he began to paint a new self-portrait. In this second self-portrait Jesus painted himself to be a prophet. Whereas the synagogue teacher was the natural setting for Jesus' ministry as a teacher, there was no institution for him to show himself to be a prophet. There were two exceptions to this: 1. Old Testament narratives about charismatic prophets, such as Moses, Elijah, and Elisha, and 2. the ministry of John the Baptist with his call to radical repentance. It is therefore no surprise that the crowds, with some uncertainty, begin to understand Jesus to be a prophet like John the Baptist or one of the prophets of old; but in the end, Jesus' self-revelation as prophet is as inadequate as his earlier self-portrait of himself as teacher. And so, as his ministry continues to unfold there comes a time for him to paint his third self-portrait. Jesus was progressively a teacher and a prophet; but he is more than these roles reveal. He is the Messiah, the Christ. Jesus' self-revelation as the Messiah, will also in the end, prove to be as inadequate as his introductory roles as teacher or as prophet, and it anticipates his climactic, fatal role as King of the Jews. But before Jesus departs from Galilee to travel to Jerusalem, he must establish his credentials as the Messiah.

Throughout his ministry, from first to last, Jesus finds himself to be caught on the horns of a dilemma. For example, if he shows himself to be a teacher without equal, some persons in the synagogue will be amazed; others will be jealous because of his popularity. Similarly, if he does the work of a prophet some will identify him to be a false prophet. In addition, should he show himself to be the Messiah, many will want to take him and make him their King, but others will seek for an opportunity to kill him. As a result,

Jesus always walks the fine line between self-revelation and hidden-ness. The miracle of the feeding of the four thousand, a parallel miracle to the earlier feeding of the five thousand, introduces the transition from his prophethood to his Messiah-ship.

4.1 Jesus Multiplies Food (8.1-21)

Twice in his narrative about Jesus in the mature period of his minis-try Mark introduces examples of Jesus feeding large crowds of fol-lowers. The first example showed Jesus to be a charismatic prophet like either Moses, or Elijah, or Elisha. Mark reports the second ex-ample perhaps to illustrate to his readership how easy it is to over-look the 'sign-message' which the miracles contain.

4.1.1 Jesus Feeds the Four Thousand (8.1-10)

Mark introduces the episode of the four thousand, reporting that Jesus calls his disciples together to discuss the feeding of the large crowd, which has gathered together to listen to him. Several mo-tives enter into his action: 1. he felt compassion for them (Mk 8.1; compare 1.41); 2. the crowd has now been with Jesus for three days (8.2a), and he knows that some of the crowd will collapse from hunger (8.2b). Many of Mark's readers, both then and now will be surprised at the disciples' spiritual blindness. This is evident in their response: 'where in this remote place can anyone get enough bread to feel them?' (8.4). They have already forgotten that Jesus, the char-ismatic prophet who is standing in their midst, just may be prepared to feed them. Nevertheless, Jesus asks them, 'How many loves do you have?' (8.5). Having taken inventory they reply, 'seven' (8.5b). The crowd is to sit down and Jesus will feed them (8.6).

The procedure follows that of the earlier miracle: Jesus breaks the loaves and the few fish they have, and the disciples distribute the food to the crowd. Afterwards, the disciples picked up the left-overs and discovered that Jesus had done what no one else in the crowd could do: feed four thousand famished men, with seven bas-kets full of leftovers (8.6-9). Having fed the multitude, Jesus and his disciples got into a boat and sailed to Dalmanutha (8.10). Apparent-ly, this second episode of feeding large crowds has silenced the dis-ciples. Certainly, there is nothing to report to their credit. Obviously, Jesus controlled his ire!

4.1.2 Some Pharisees Ask For a Sign (8.11-13)

Mark now juxtaposes a short narrative about the Pharisees to his report about feeding of the four thousand (Mk 8.1-10). Their motive is 'to test him' (8.11). Mark has used the same word 'test' at 1.13 to report that in the wilderness after Jesus' baptism, Satan 'tested' Jesus. Apparently, Mark is implying that these Pharisees are here continuing the work of Satan. The test is for Jesus to give, 'a sign from heaven' (8.11). This term, 'a sign from heaven', means 'a sign from God'. When Jesus multiplied a little food (i.e. seven loaves of bread) into enough food to feed a crowd of four thousand men, he has just done what the Pharisees have asked for – given them a sign from heaven, from God. Therefore, Jesus asks rhetorically, 'Why does this generation ask for a sign?' (8.12). And just as Jesus refused to yield to Satan's test, so now he refuses to perform miracles on demand (apart from those miracles that come from God's will and purpose). Having refused to become embroiled in this test, Jesus, in a manner of speaking, turned his back on them and got into a boat with his disciples, 'and crossed to the other side'. Clearly, this episode teaches that while miracles make believers out of believers, they often fail to make believers out of unbelievers.

4.1.3 Jesus Warns About the Yeast of the Pharisees (8.14-21)

The setting for this episode is the crossing of the Sea of Galilee after Jesus has turned his back on the Pharisees who had tested him. While they are crossing the lake, the disciples realize that they have just one loaf of bread with them. Mark reports, 'they had forgotten to bring bread, except for one loaf' (Mk 8.14). In this context, Jesus warns, 'be careful ... watch out for the yeast of Pharisees (8.15; compare also 8.11-13). He also warns them against the yeast of Herod, perhaps an echo of the alliance between the Pharisees and the Herodians, which Mark has reported in 3.6. The disciples, 'discussed this with one another' (8.16a), and clearly, didn't understand Jesus' warning. All that they can think about is bread for the stomach, but Jesus is thinking about another, higher level of meaning.

From now on, Jesus is going to press the disciples to move beyond their current, inadequate level of understanding. Very pointedly, he asks, 'why are you talking about having no bread?' (8.17a). Mincing no words, he continued to press them:

Do you still not see or understand?
Are your hearts hardened?
Do you have eyes, but fail to see, and ears to hear, but fail to hear?
And don't you remember?

Jesus could very well be talking to the Pharisees here, but he isn't. He is talking to his disciples, whom he has earlier called 'so dull' (7.18). Now he asks, 'When I broke the five loaves for the five thousand, how many basketfuls of pieces did you pick up?' (8.19). 'Twelve', they replied. 'Jesus continued', asking, 'and when I broke the seven loaves for the four thousand, how many basketfuls of pieces did you pick up?' (8.20). They answered, 'seven'. Finally, Jesus asked, 'Do you not still understand?' (8.21).

The disciples have no answers for Jesus. They do have hardened hearts, that is, they are spiritually insensitive to the meaning of Jesus' ministry. They do have eyes to see Jesus' miracles, but only at the level of his compassion, but not as signs of his personhood. They have heard Jesus' teachings, but they always have to ask for an explanation. In spite of studying under the best teacher in the world, the disciples still don't understand, even though they still remember. The lack of understanding illustrates that understanding is not always a matter of intellectual ability; it may be a matter of spiritual sensitivity. The answer to Jesus' challenging rebuke to his hard-hearted disciples is one more miracle – an enacted parable that brings all of the strands of these questions together.

4.2 Jesus Gives Insight (8.22-30)

The episode of the feeding of the 'four thousand' and its aftermath has exposed a lack of spiritual sensitivity on the part of the disciples. They have earned the rebuke, which Jesus gives them for this inability to understand, to see and to hear, but they do remember, and Jesus' healing of the blind man in Bethsaida becomes a positive teaching and learning experience. The following comments illustrate the spiritual progress of the disciples.

A – *Spiritually* the disciples have eyes to see, but do not see (8.18).

B – *Physically* the blind man in Bethsaida has eyes but does not see (8.22).

B₁ – *Physically* Jesus bestows his healing touch, progressively step by step. The result is an out-of-focus healing. Once again, Jesus puts his hands on the man's eyes and this healing touch puts everything into focus (8.24)

A₁ – *Spiritually* the disciples have been seeing Jesus 'out-of-focus'. The progressive restoration of the blind man's sight is the model for the new spiritual insight given to the disciples. Now they begin to see spiritual things clearly.

After leaving Bethsaida, Jesus and his disciples travel to Caesarea Philippi. This is not the port city, Caesarea Maritima, which was the seat of Roman government in Judea. Caesarea Philippi is in northern Galilee, at the base of Mt. Hermon, which is covered in snow year round. It is also the center for the worship of the Greek god, Pan. In this setting, Jesus asks his disciples about his reputation in northern Galilee (8.25). As happened in other parts of Galilee, here also Jesus is reputed to be 'John the Baptist, others say Elijah, and still others one of the prophets' (8.18; compare 6.14, 15). Now, having recently witnessed his miracles of progressive healing (8.22-26), the disciples are beginning to see clearly. When Jesus asks the disciples, 'What about you … who do you say that I am' (8.28). Peter has the answer: 'You [Jesus] are the Christ' (8.29). Progressive revelation has brought the disciples to understand that Jesus is more than a great charismatic prophet – he is their long awaited Messiah, but it is not now the time to make it public (8.30).

4.3 Jesus Predicts His Death (8.31–9.1)
It may not be the right time to reveal to the public that Jesus is the Messiah, but it is not too early for Jesus to begin to teach his disciples about his approaching death. As they have been reading Mark's narrative, alert Bible readers will have been looking for hints and signs about this. Indeed, Jesus began his teaching ministry under the shadow of the cross. First, he is accused of blasphemy, which is a sin punishable by death (Mk 2.7). Following this Jesus heals a man on the Sabbath, and the teachers of the law begin to plot with the Herodians about how they might destroy him (3.6). If being a teacher invites such murderous hatred (thinly disguised as keeping the law), how much more will Jesus, who has been doing the work of a prophet be in danger of being killed. However, his self-portrait as the Messiah will see his destiny end in the martyr's death. And his

disciples need to know and understand this unthinkable fact. Unthinkable? Yes! But these are the essential facts of the Christian message of Good News. And, of course, this is the primary subject of Mark's Gospel.

Knowing that his disciples are likely to misunderstand his messianic mission, 'he began to teach them that the Son of Man must suffer many things' (Mk 8.31a). This teaching includes the fact that he will be rejected by a coalition of secular and religious leaders, including 'the elders, chief priests, and teachers of the law' (8.31b). These 'many things' which Jesus begins to teach about include the paradoxical fact that 'he must be killed, and after three days rise again' (8.31c). Mark observes, 'he [Jesus] spoke plainly about this' (8.31c). Certainly, for once Peter understood what Jesus meant, and this portrait of a suffering Messiah did not fit his expectations of a military, royal Messiah. So, 'Peter took him aside and began to rebuke him' (8.32). Seeing that Peter was influencing the other disciples, 'Jesus rebuked Peter' (8.33). Jesus' rebuke of Peter is some of the harshest words spoken anywhere in Scripture: 'Get behind me, Satan' (8.33). At Peter's moment of highest insight, confessing Jesus to be the Messiah (8.29), Peter also reveals the lowest depths of human understanding – wanting to divert Jesus from his redemptive ministry on the Cross. Jesus graciously softens his rebuke: 'You do not have in mind the things of God [Messiahship is about redemptive suffering], but the things of man [Israel's Messiah will be an all-conquering, David-like Warrior]' (8.33).

After this double rebuke, Jesus 'called the crowd to him, along with the disciples' to teach about discipleship (8.34). He teaches that discipleship has the same cost as Messiahship. In other words, just as Jesus will suffer and be killed, so to be his disciples, they must take up their cross – be prepared to lose their lives (8.35); however, there is victory in losing one's life for the sake of the gospel. Though Jesus will be killed, he will be glorified (8.38). Even before that, the Kingdom of God will come in power (9.1).

4.4 Jesus is Transfigured (9.2-13)

Six days before being transfigured Jesus had promised his disciples that some of them would see the Kingdom of God come in power. This sounds as if the coming of the Kingdom – whatever that means – will be an explosive, dramatic event. But, Mark reports what actually happened as if it was a day-to-day event, rather than the revelation of the coming of the Kingdom of God. Not only does Mark strip the event of much of its dynamic drama, but he also reports it with utmost economy of words.

Though Mark has stripped his narrative of its inherent drama, he describes the event as if it were a Theophany with 'glorification' sidelights. The 'glorification' sidelights include Moses' experiences on Mt. Sinai (Exod. 24.13-18; 33.12-30, *et al*), and Elijah's sudden ascension (2 Kgs 2.10, 11). The transfiguration happens six days after Peter's confession that Jesus is the Messiah/Christ (Mk 9.2). At this time, Jesus takes his inner circle of disciples, namely, Peter, James, and John with him. Together they climb a high mountain, which remains unidentified in the narrative, but which is most likely to be Mt. Hermon, whose peaks are clad with snow year round.[16] As Jesus has done before he has sought out a lonely place (for prayer? Compare Mk 1.35, 3.13; 6.46). The verb, which with two exceptions is used exclusively here, is *metamorphoo* (μεταμορφόω), which comes into the English language as the word 'metamorphosis' (compare Rom. 12.2; 2 Cor. 2.18). Jesus' transfiguration is tangible, based in the observation that 'his clothes became dazzling white' (9.3). For emphasis, Mark adds that these were 'whiter than anyone in the world could bleach them' (9.3). As Jesus undergoes this experience of metamorphosis, 'there appeared before them Elijah and Moses who were talking with Jesus' (9.4). But though Mark is Peter's 'son' and 'scribe' (1 Pet. 5.13),[17] he reveals no secrets about the subject(s) of their conversation.

Never at a loss for words (almost!), Peter blurts out, 'Rabbi [which means teacher], it is good for us to be here' (Mk 9.5). Peter was often a take-charge kind of leader, and, true to form, he proposes, 'let us put up three shelters – one for you, one for Moses, and one for Elijah' (9.5). The word that is translated as 'shelters' is *skenas*, (σκηνάς), which in the Exodus account is used to identify the 'Tabernacle'. This word identified God's portable dwelling place on earth (Exod. 40.34). Mark informs his readers, parenthetically, that 'he [Peter] did not know what to say, they were so frightened' (9.5).

In spite of Peter's ill-advised proposal, a cloud appeared and enveloped them such as happened when Moses dedicated the Taber-

---

[16] The other option is Mt. Tabor.
[17] Eusebius, *Eccl. Hist.*, 6.14.

nacle (Exod. 40.1-34). We may identify this cloud as, 'The cloud of his presence', which was with Israel in the Exodus (Exod. 13.21). Thus, the appearance of this cloud on Mt. Hermon is a theophany (a tangible experience of God's presence). God has a special, private message (9.9) for these three disciples. This message echoes the voice from heaven when Jesus was baptized. Compare:

> You are my Son, whom I love, with you I am well pleased (1.11).
> This is my Son, whom I love. Listen to him (9.7).

The first message was spoken at the Jordan River when Jesus was baptized by John, the second here on Mt. Hermon. The first message consecrated and commissioned Jesus for his ministry in Galilee, the second commissions Jesus for a new phase, soon to be revealed. Mark's readers will soon read that this is about leaving Galilee and travelling up to Jerusalem (10.1–11.11). The Theophanic voice commands the apostolic trio to 'listen to him', which identifies Jesus to be the prophet like Moses (compare Deut. 18.15).

Having now met the two prophets, whom it has been his duty to emulate, i.e. Moses and Elijah, Jesus' transfiguration scene ends as it began. Suddenly Jesus is alone with his three disciples (9.8), but there are still two loose ends to tie up. The first loose end relates to the so-called 'Messianic Secret' which Mark introduced in his first portrait (note Mk 1.24, 44). Mark now reports, 'As they were coming down the mountain Jesus gave them orders not to tell anyone what they had seen until the Son of Man had risen from the dead' (9.9). This will be the last time that Jesus will command silence. God has just recently commanded the disciples to 'listen to him'. Paradoxically, this is the first time that the command not to tell anyone is obeyed. However, they are still mystified about what 'rising from the dead' means – a mystification that even Jesus' resurrection from the dead did not immediately dispel (9.10b). The second loose end is about the coming of (eschatological) Elijah before that great and dreadful day of the Lord comes (Mal. 4.5). The presence of the prophet Elijah on the Mount of Transfiguration has no doubt triggered their curiosity. The prophecy about Elijah is an enigma because John the Baptist and Jesus each fulfills different aspects of the prophecy. The Gospels do not eliminate the enigma (9.12, 13).

Earlier in this commentary, I have referred to the narrative strategy called 'inclusio'. The term describes the strategy of introducing a concluding block of narrative by ending a section of material using the same or similar imagery or terminology, which was used at the beginning. Mark uses Jesus' experience of the two signature miracles in order to delimit his ministry in Galilee (1.9–9.50). The following chart illustrates this, and gives a sense of completeness to what was initiated by the first theophany. It also introduces a new direction with Jesus giving a fourth and final self-portrait – revealing that he is the (rejected) King of the Jews.

Two Theophanies: Jesus Ministers in Galilee (1.9–9.50)

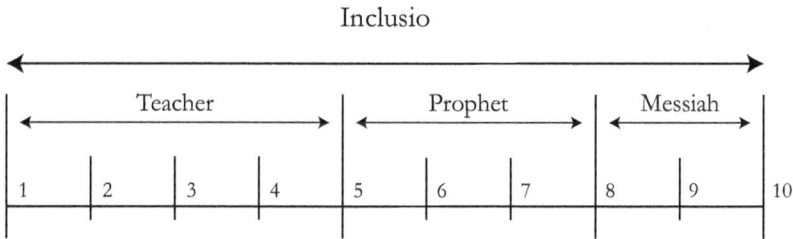

Inclusio

	Teacher				Prophet			Messiah	
1	2	3	4	5	6	7	8	9	10

Theophany (1.9-11) voices from Heaven Beginning of Jesus Ministry in Galilee

Theophany (9.2-13). voices from a Cloud End of Jesus Ministry in Galilee

4.5 Jesus Heals a Boy with an Unclean Spirit (9.14-29)

Earlier in Jesus' self-portrait as the prophet, Jesus had performed a short series of signature miracles, specifically he cast out demons and he healed a woman who suffered a twelve year-long incurable affliction (Mk 5.1-34). Soon after this Jesus sent out his disciples, who are 'prophets-in-training' (6.7-13). Naturally, Jesus, their teacher, expected them to reproduce his prophetic words (1.14) and his prophetic works (1.22-28; 5.1-34). Of course, Jesus *did not* expect his disciples to do these things on their own. Therefore, for example, he gave them *power* over evil spirits (6.7). In due time, they returned to Jesus and reported, 'they drove out many demons and anointed many people with oil and healed them' (6.13). But now, as Jesus and Peter, James and John return to the disciples, who are awaiting their return, they find a different kind of scene. Rather than hearing something positive, they find that the other disciples are embroiled in an argument with the teachers of the law (9.14).

The cause of this argument is that disciples as prophets-in-training (Mk 6.7-13) who had cast out 'many demons' have now, in Jesus' absence, been unable to cast out one evil spirit. The father of the boy who is possessed by the evil spirit explains, 'I asked your disciples to drive out the spirit, but they could not' (9.17). Jesus, who had just returned from the glory of his metamorphosis experience, is naturally frustrated and exclaims, 'O unbelieving generations, how long should I stay with you? ... Bring the boy to me' (9.19). Jesus encourages the father to believe, saying, 'everything is possible for him who believes' (9.20). The father exclaims, 'I do believe!' This must be true or he wouldn't have brought the boy to Jesus in the first place, but in the very act of affirming his faith a seed of doubt springs up in his heart and mind, and so he implores Jesus, 'help me overcome my unbelief' (9.24). As a crowd continues to gather, Jesus acts. He rebukes the spirit, saying, 'I command you to come out of him and never enter him again' (9.25). Jesus then lifts the boy to his feet and he stood up, forever free (9.27).

The disciples do not understand the discrepancy between their earlier experience (6.13) and their present inability to cast out the evil spirit. When they are alone with Jesus they ask him, 'Why couldn't we drive it out?' (9.28). The answer is, 'This kind can come out only by prayer' (9.29). Note that some translations read, 'by prayer and fasting'. In this instance, the disciples have been confronted with the failure to pray. So, they were out of touch with God. Possibly, they had also failed to fast. So, they lacked certain levels of self-discipline. One commentator has observed, 'only prayerfulness and strict self-disciple can make a man spiritually competent to deal with such situations'.[18]

4.6 Jesus Foretells His Death and Resurrection (9.30-50)

4.1.6.1 Jesus Announces His Death and Resurrection (9.30-33)

Time marches on. The transfiguration will soon show that it will be a turning point in Jesus' life and now, for a second time, he announces his death and resurrection. Recall that the first announcement followed Peter's confession that Jesus is the Christ (Mk 8.29).

---

[18] Cranfield, *Mark*, p. 313.

At that time, Jesus began to teach his disciples about his death at the hands of the Jewish leaders, both sacred and secular, and his resurrection three days later (8.31, 32). After the transfiguration, Jesus travels through Galilee to escape the crowds – something that almost took a miracle to achieve (9.30). As his death approached (8.31, 32), he needed more private teaching time with his disciples. Mark reports that he again taught his disciples, 'the Son of Man is going to be betrayed into the hands of men' (9.30). It is the act of 'betrayal' which distinguishes this announcement about his death from the first announcement. Now, for the second time, he states plainly, 'they will kill him, and after three days he will rise' (9.31). Mark, no doubt as Peter's scribe, once again emphasizes 'that they did not understand what he meant' (compare 8.17, 21). However, they, 'were afraid to ask him about it' (9.23), perhaps anticipating a further possible rebuke for their inability to understand (8.17, 21, 32, 33).

4.1.6.2 Jesus Teaches About Greatness (9.33-36)

Having passed through Galilee, they came to Capernaum (Mk 9.33). When he has a private time with his disciples, he confronts them, asking, 'what were you arguing about on the road?' (9.33). The disciples kept quiet, they were silent, 'because on the way they had argued about who is the greatest' (9.34). This is a teachable moment, and Jesus seized the opportunity. He reminded the disciples that values in the Kingdom turn those of the world upside down, for 'if anyone wants to be first, he must be the very last, and the servant of all' (9.36). He illustrated this by picking up a child, who is insignificant in many contexts, but the greatest when identified with God.

4.1.6.3 Jesus Teaches About Allies and Enemies (9.38-41)

Mark has focused his narrative primarily on Jesus and on the twelve, who are teachers and prophets-in-training. It is, therefore, easy to forget that from the earliest days of Jesus' ministry he has many other disciples. On one occasion, he called his disciples together, and from within this larger group, he called the Twelve disciples to be with him (Mk 3.13). After the transfiguration narrative, John – no doubt thinking that Jesus will approve his action – reports that the Twelve had forbidden a man to cast out demons in Jesus' name, 'because he was not one of us' (9.38). John reveals that the twelve

disciples think that they and they alone of Jesus' five hundred disciples (1 Cor. 15.6) have been authorized by Jesus to minister on his
behalf. But this is not so.

Jesus responds to John's report teaching the twelve two lessons.
First, 'the one who ministers in his name cannot at the same time
say bad things about him' (9.39). In other words, one's actions show
that he or she is an ally and not an enemy. Second, Jesus claims,
'whoever is not against us is for us' (9.40). Such a one, who may do
nothing more than give a cup of cold water in Jesus' name, will receive a reward (9.41).

4.1.6.4 Jesus Teaches About Causing Others to Sin (9.42-50)

Many of those (who believe in Jesus), are like the anonymous person who cast out demons in Jesus' name and are the 'little ones'
who are numbered among Jesus' many disciples. The disciples need
to be 'encouraging' them to minister and not causing them to sin by
discouraging them (9.43). Causing a little one who believes to sin
(for any reason) bears unintended consequences of the most serious kind. For that one, it would be better to be cast into the sea and
drown than to cause another to sin. Even the disciple who sins faces grave consequences. Jesus taught:

> If your hand causes you to sin, cut it off
> If you foot causes you to sin, cut it off, and
> If your eye causes your to sin, pluck it out.

In these examples the hand, foot, and/or eye are symbolic language
symbolizing what a person does, where a person goes, and/or what
a person desires. The church has always believed Jesus' language to
be metaphorical. And even at its least extreme it must be balanced
by the amazing grace of God – that even the disciple or believer
who sins is free from the condemnation which she or he might de-
serve (Rom. 8.1, 31-35; 1 Jn 2.1, 2). The lesson, which disciples of
every age can take away from Jesus' teaching, is that one's sin or another's is not a trifling matter.

Finally, Jesus teaches about salt. Jesus teaches the disciples that
everyone will be salted with fire (9.49). He expects his disciples to
remember and to understand (Mk 8.17-21) that the law required
that sacrifices were to be salted (Lev. 2.13; Ezek. 43.24). The idea
here is that the disciples are to be sacrifices to God (Rom. 12.1).

This is not only a sacrificial practice, but it is also domestic imagery. The disciples are to be salt in the world, which left to itself would go bad (Mt. 5.13).

MARK 10.1–15.47

JESUS MINISTERS IN JERUSALEM

JESUS MINISTERS IN JERUSALEM (10.1–15.47): JESUS IS THE KING OF THE JEWS

Jesus began his ministry in Galilee, where he revealed himself to be a teacher, the Prophet to Jews and Gentiles, and, finally as the Christ (1.21–9.50). Throughout his time in Galilee, he evoked mixed responses to his words and works. On the one hand, needy individuals, such as the leper and the crippled man (1.40–2.12), and the crowds of common people approved of him (1.28; 2.12, *et al*). Many of his followers even thought that he might be John the Baptist, Elijah, or one of the other prophets risen from the dead (6.14; 8.29). On the other hand, those who were the religious elite, such as the Teachers of the Law and the Pharisees, disapproved of his attitude towards their traditions, and, on occasion, looked upon him with murderous hatred (2.7; 3.6). However, Jesus' destiny will not be determined in Galilee. For Jesus to reveal himself to be the King of the Jews, he must go up to Jerusalem – the city of Melchizedek, King and priest, of David, the warrior prophet, of Solomon, the wise administrator, and the Davidic dynasty.

Ultimately, Jesus is the Christ – after the pattern of anointed Kingship. However, Kingship is necessarily identified with Judah and Jerusalem. Therefore, at this point in Mark's Gospel, and also for the first time in the gospel, Jesus journeys to Judea and Jerusalem. There, with a wicked twist, he will be crowned the (rejected) King of the Jews. Not only did the coalition of Jewish leadership, e.g. elders, priests, and teachers of the law, *et al*, reject him but, as an act of judicial murder, they will kill him (8.31; 9.31, 10.33). Mark tells this part of Jesus' story in two stages: 1. Jesus journeys to Jerusalem (10.1–11.11), and he ministers in Jerusalem (11.12–16.20).

5.1 Jesus Journeys to Jerusalem (10.1–11.11)

As the Jewish Passover season approaches, Jesus and his disciples join a larger group of devout Jews who are making the annual journey to Jerusalem. Some Jews will take the road through Samaria, but Jesus and the others will take the road along the Jordan River to Jericho, where they will turn west for the climb up out of the river valley to Bethany on the Mt. of Olives. Leaving Bethany, they will circle the Mt. of Olives and approach the city across the brook of Kedron, with the Temple before them in all of its splendor. The pilgrimage from Galilee normally takes from three to five days, but this isn't a normal crowd. As Mark reports, this isn't a normal pilgrimage. Jesus leads the way – as if he has a purpose greater than Passover celebration. In addition, the disciples are *astonished* (at Jesus' demeanor, which is probably unusual). Many in the larger group are *afraid* (10.32). Jesus takes advantage of the astonishment and the fear to give the crowd some final teaching. The first of his subjects is the issue of divorce.

5.1.1 Jesus Teaches About Divorce (10.1-12)

Mark reports, 'as was his custom, he taught them [i.e. the crowd]' (10.1). Likely many in this crowd chose to journey with Jesus to Jerusalem for the additional benefit of his teaching, but this setting also made him vulnerable, and 'some Pharisees came and tested him' (10.2a). Mark's alert readers will remember that twice before he has reported that Jesus was being tested (1.13; by Satan; 8.11-13, by the Pharisees). Mark's use of this verb is interesting. It might mean that these Pharisees, despite their façade of righteousness, are doing Satan's work. In addition, it shows that their motive is not one of serious, unhypocritical enquiry. The test is the much-debated question, 'Is it lawful for a man to divorce his wife?' (10.2b). This test puts Jesus on the horns of a dilemma, for whichever way he answers those of the opposite side of the question will be unhappy with him.

But, Jesus is not about to let himself be trapped. Therefore, he answers their question by asking them a question, 'What did Moses command you?', he replied (10.3). This is a question about what the law, i.e. Scripture, might say on the subject of divorce. It is also a challenge to these Pharisees about the authority of their tradition – Scripture vs. Tradition. They replied, 'Moses permitted a man to write a certificate of divorce and send her away' (10.4). Clearly, these Pharisees are indifferent about 'what Moses says'. Equally clear, they are asking Jesus about which Rabbi, namely R. Shammai or R. Hillel, gives the correct teaching.

R. Shammai – permitted divorce for the reason of unchastity.
R. Hillel – permitted divorce for trivial matters (e.g. because the wife spoiled a dish [i.e. a meal]), and
R. Akiba – permitted divorce if he found another (women) fairer than his wife (*Gittin* 9.10).

Quoting Gen. 2.24, 25, Jesus lets Moses, i.e. Scripture, answer the Pharisees. Jesus makes three points in his answer. 1. Divorce was a concession from God because of their sin (Deut. 24.1; Mk 10.5). 2. The theology of creation is marriage, not divorce, unity, not separation (10.6-8). 3. Man is to live in light of God's creative purpose (Gen. 2.24); not in light of God's concessive purpose (Deut. 24.1).

The disciples, who, unlike the Pharisees, have had no formal training in the traditions, 'asked Jesus about this' (10.10). Jesus answered, 'anyone who [capriciously] divorces his wife, as the rabbinic traditions allow, and marries another woman commits adultery against her' (10.11). Similarly, 'if a woman divorces her husband and marries another man, she commits adultery' (10.12). In other words, a bill of divorce does not separate a husband and wife, though adultery does separate what God has joined together. To live after the rabbinic fashion of frivolous divorces is adultery (10.12). Mark's readership can take away two points from this. The first is that 'Moses' (i.e. Scripture) is more authoritative than the Traditions of the Elders. The second lesson is that humans are sinners, and as long as sin is allowed to taint a marriage, there will be divorces.

5.1.2 Jesus Teaches About Entering the Kingdom as a Child Enters (10.13-16)

As Jesus, his disciples, and the crowd continue along the road to Jericho and Jerusalem, 'People were bringing little children to Jesus to have him touch them' (10.13a). The 'touch' which they are seeking is first and foremost, the touch of blessing. Secondarily, some children may also need the touch of healing. The disciples are indignant about this. They must have thought that Jesus, leading the crowd of Passover pilgrims, had more important people to talk to and more important things to do and they rebuked the parents of these children (10.13b). So, the disciples are indignant about the interruption from these parents, but, in turn, Jesus is indignant about the attitude of his disciples (10.14).

Speaking to his disciples, Jesus commanded, 'Let the little children come to me, and do not hinder them' (10.14b). The disciples do not care about the children, but Jesus, whose mission it is to establish the Kingdom of God (1.15), insists that the 'Kingdom of God belongs to such as these' (10.14c). In fact, these little children model for adults the way for them to enter the Kingdom, just as these little children trust their heavenly Father. There is no other way to be happy in the Kingdom than to trust and obey. Having taught his disciples about children in the Kingdom of God, 'he took the children in his arms, put his hands on them and blessed them' (10.16). There were many happy parents in the crowd that day.

5.1.3 Jesus Teaches, Do Not Enter the Kingdom as a Rich Man (10.17-31)

A journey on foot, such as the one from Galilee to Jerusalem, is characterized by many stops and starts. The episode of the rich man happens at one of the many starts. Mark reports, 'as Jesus started on his way a man ran up to Jesus and fell on his knees before him' (10.17). He addresses Jesus as he would address any other teacher: 'Good Teacher' (10.17b), and then engages Jesus in a discussion. He asks, 'What must I do to inherit eternal life?' (10.17c). Testing the sincerity of the man, Jesus brushes him off. If all the man wants is what a rabbi can provide, Jesus rejects the greeting (10.18), 'Why do you call me good?', Jesus asks (10.18). He also affirms, 'No one is good – except God alone' (10.18b). He seems to be saying that the man should be asking God this kind of question, for determining eternal life is God's prerogative. In fact, not the Rabbis but God has already given the answer: 'Do not murder, do not commit adultery, do not steal, *et al*' (10.18c). The man has learned his lesson well – and now addresses Jesus as 'Teacher', having dropped the 'good' in 'good teacher' (10.20). 'Teacher', he declared, 'all these I have kept since I was a boy' (10.20). As another Jew of the same generation as this man once wrote, 'as for legalistic righteousness, faultless' (Phil. 3.6). And he too craved something more than legalistic righteousness.

There is something very special about this man, for only the second or third time the gospel reports, 'Jesus ... loved him' – as he must have loved the young Paul, who, 'in regard to the law [was] a Pharisee' (Phil. 3.5). Jesus discerned the man's weakness. He must do more than keep the commandments; he must also develop a sacrificial attitude towards others who are more needy than he is. Jesus urges him, 'Go, sell everything you have and give it to the poor' (10.21). In other words, Jesus is telling him to value 'treasures in heaven' more than he values 'treasures on earth' (10.21b). However, in the end, love of treasures on earth was his downfall; 'At this the man's face fell' (10.22). In spite of his moral rectitude and his longing for heaven, 'his present wealth derailed him' (10.22).

As the man walked away, Jesus said to his disciples, 'How hard it is for the rich to enter the Kingdom of God!' (10.23). Mark reports that Jesus' 'disciples were amazed' (10.23). Their amazement makes it probable that at some points in their young lives they coveted some 'this' or 'that', which wealth could provide, but Jesus reaffirms this principle, 'Children, how hard it is to enter the Kingdom of God' (10.24a). In fact, Jesus observes, 'it is easier for a camel to go through the eye of a needle than for a rich man to enter the Kingdom of God' (10.24b). Some Bible readers interpret the camel/needle metaphor to describe low gates in city walls, which require the camel to shuffle through on its knees, but this is difficult, though it is not impossible. Therefore, I interpret Jesus' metaphor to be about a camel going through the eye of a sewing needle – which is impossible! 'Who can be saved?', the disciples exclaim in amazement. Jesus explains, 'with man this is impossible' – wealth is not a spiritual asset. However, Jesus assures the disciples, though 'with man this is impossible ... but not with God; all things are possible with God' (10.27).

Consciously or unconsciously, Peter wants Jesus to affirm the disciples. So, he abruptly reminds Jesus, 'We have left everything to follow you!' (10.28). 'I tell you the truth', Jesus replied, 'no one who has left home, or brother or sisters or mother ... for me [Jesus] and the gospel will fail to receive a hundred times as much in this present age' (10.29). However, they will receive the bad with the good, namely, 'persecutions' and in the age to come, eternal life (10.30). This episode began with an anonymous man asking Jesus, 'What must I do to inherit eternal life?' (10.17). It concludes with Jesus' answer: Leave everything for me and the gospel. To follow Jesus is a reversal of human expectations, for 'many who are first will be last, and the last first' (10.31).

5.1.4 Jesus Predicts His Death (10.32-34)

After Jesus has taught about 'eternal life, they continued along the way up to Jerusalem' (10.32). Many in the crowd have made this pilgrimage before, but this time it is different. Jesus led the crowd; the disciples were astonished; and the crowd that followed were afraid. Many of these devout Jews discerned that this was becoming a journey of unprecedented destiny. Now and for the third time, Jesus announces to his disciples what will happen to him: 'the Son of Man will be betrayed to the chief priests and the teachers of the law' (10.33). The new element in this announcement is that, having condemned him to death, the chief priests, 'will hand him over to the Gentiles. They will kill him with uttermost brutality – they will mock him and spit on him, and kill him' (10.34a). In spite of this treatment, 'three days later he will rise' (10.34b).

5.1.5 Jesus Teaches About Messiahship (10.35-45)

Hearing Jesus repeatedly announce that after being killed and that he will rise again (8.31; 9.31; 10.34), James and John came to him (10.35). They have a request to make of Jesus, 'What do you want me to do for you', he asked (10.36). When Jesus comes into his royal glory, 'Let one of us sit on your right and the other on your left' (10.37). Mincing no words, Jesus tells them, 'You don't know what you are asking' (10.38). Even though they can drink the cup of suffering, which Jesus will drink and will be baptized with the baptism of suffering and which Jesus will be baptized, he does not have the authority to grant their request (10.39). The places on the right and left hand 'belong to those for whom they have been prepared' (10.39, 40).

James and John have been talking privately to Jesus, but, as often happens, word gets out. Mark reports the reaction of the other apostles. Simply put, they were indignant (10.40). Perhaps, some of the others kicked themselves for not thinking about, or not having the courage to ask for a place of honor for themselves, but this is to indulge in idle and unprofitable speculation. What isn't up to speculation is the lesson about discipleship and messiahship. The first lesson is about the use of power and lordship in leadership. Jesus has observed, 'that those who are regarded as rulers of Gentiles lord it over them' (10.42a); that is, they act as 'lords'. Similarly, high officials exercise authority over them (10.42b). However, 'it is *not with you*' (10.43). Those among Jesus' disciples who seek lordship and authority are thinking/acting like Gentiles (i.e. unbelievers). Instead, Jesus' followers, especially his apostles, led by the qualities of *servanthood* (*diakonos*, διάκονος, see Acts 1.25) and as a *slave* (*doulos*, δοῦλος, Rom. 1.1). The contrast between these two patterns is stark. It is also a stinging indictment against those among Jesus' followers who abuse their power and lead God's people after the Gentile pattern. Rome illustrates that Gentile power is often not gentle.

Jesus leads by the same qualities. Thus, *even* the Son of Man did not come to be served (*diakoneo*, διακονέω); compare Acts 1.25), but to serve (*diakoneo*). He will serve to the ultimate level: to Jesus service means that he will give his life as a ransom for many. The English word 'ransom' translates the Greek word, *lutron* (λύτρον), and it is used to identify the price paid to free a slave from his or her bondage.[19] It is used only one other time in the New Testament (Mt. 20.28). The Greek word *anti* (ἀντί) is 'for', and it conveys the ideas of 'exchange' and 'substitution'. Jesus' teaching therefore, describes Messiahship as 'serving, giving, paying a price as a substitute for others'. Similarly, he defines discipleship to be about serving, giving, and paying the price for the benefit of others. All in all, Jesus' teaching to James and John and the rest of the apostles, is that following him, even at the highest level of ministry, is about serving others, and is *not* about being served, taking, and paying the price for the benefit of one's self.

5.1.6 Jesus Heals Blind Bartimaeus (10.46-52)
The journey to Jerusalem now reaches its final stage. This is Jericho, and from here, Jerusalem is a one-day, arduous climb from 1290 ft below sea level at Jericho to 2200 ft above sea level at Jerusalem. Jesus and the disciples leave Jericho as part of a large crowd (10.46a). As they leave Jericho, they pass a blind beggar who is 'sitting by the roadside, begging' (10.46b). As the crowd passes by, he learns that Jesus of Nazareth is part of the crowd (10.47). At this

---

[19] Walter Bauer *et al.*, *A Greek-English Lexicon of the New Testament and Other Early Christian Literature* (Chicago: University of Chicago Press, 2d edn, 1979), p. 483.

news, 'he began to shout, Jesus, "Son of David" have mercy on me' (10.47). And so, it is here at Jericho that for the first time in his narrative, Mark reports that Jesus has begun to be identified with David. Many in the crowd try to silence the beggar, but the more they try the more insistent he shouts, 'Son of David, have mercy on me' (10.47).

The man's shouting carried through the noise of the crowd. Jesus hears it, and stopped, and instructed, 'Call him' (10.49). They, then, 'called to the blind man, "cheer up! On your feet! He's calling you"' (10.49). Excited, he threw his cloak aside, jumped up and came to Jesus (10.50). Some beggars might have asked for a generous gift, but this beggar knows that Jesus can do what no one in the crowd can do – heal him. So, when Jesus asks, 'what do you want me to do for you he replied, "Rabbi, I want to see"' (10.51). Jesus then dismisses the blind beggar, 'Go ... your faith has healed you' (10.52). Mark concludes this narrative, reporting, and immediately he receives his sight and followed Jesus along the road (10.52).

5.1.7 Jesus Enters Jerusalem (11.1-11)
After the arduous climb from Jericho through the wilderness they come to the village of Bethphage and Bethany on the southeast slope of the Mount of Olives (11.1). From here, Jesus will stage his dramatic and fateful entry into Jerusalem (11.1). At this point, as his action shows he is deliberately, consciously taking on the role of Solomon entering Jerusalem to be crowned as David's successor (11.2-7; 1 Kgs 1.38). To do this, he must have a colt/donkey, and he sends two disciples to fetch one (11.2, 3). They find a colt as Jesus had directed and return to Jesus, who then mounts and rides around the Mount of Olives, from southeast to the southwest. As they circle the Mount of Olives, Jerusalem, dominated by the Temple lies before them (11.4-7). The first century Jewish historian, Josephus, describes the splendor that meets the eye.

The exterior of the building (Temple) wanted nothing that could astound either mind or eye. For being covered on all sides with massive plates of gold, the sun was no sooner up that it radiated so fiercely a flash of light that persons straining to look at it were compelled to avert their eyes, as from the solar rays. To approaching strangers, it appeared from a distance like a snow-clad mountain; for all that was not overlaid with gold was the purest white.[20]

This magnificent scene was compounded by the 'red-carpet' welcome that was accorded to Jesus: 'many spread their clothes on the road, and others cut down leafy branches from the trees and spread them on the road' (11.8). He entered Jerusalem accompanied by the spontaneous singing of Psalm 118 – one of the Passover Psalms. Mark records part of the psalm in his narrative, the people shouted:

> Hosanna!
> Blessed is he who comes in the name of the Lord!
> Blessed is the coming Kingdom of Our Father David!
> Hosanna in the highest! (Ps. 118.25, 26).

Thus, this setting – the Temple, the Solomon-like coronation, the Psalm announcing the coming of David's Kingdom – inevitably evokes the expectation that Jesus is Israel's royal Messiah. The triumphal entry seems to be a denial of his own predictions of his death. He had taught, 'that the Son of Man must suffer many things, and be rejected by the elders and chief priests and scribes, and be killed' (8.31; cf. 9.31). Moreover, even as he and his disciples had traveled toward Jerusalem, Jesus had informed them, "Behold, we are going up to Jerusalem, and the Son of Man will be betrayed to the chief priests and to the scribes; and they will condemn him to death and deliver him to the Gentiles; and they will mock him, and scourge him, and spit on him, and kill him' (10.33-34). Yet Jesus leaves the Temple and returns to Bethany. In leaving the Temple, Jesus turns his back upon the messianic expectations of the crowd. Therefore, as events unfold, in a few days this same crowd will reject him as their Messianic King. If he would not conform to their expectations for a messiah who would overthrow the Romans, they did not want him at all. Frustrated, disillusioned, disappointed with him, they turn on him and judicially murder him.

---

[20] Josephus, *Wars*, 5.222-24.

5.2 Jesus Ministers in Jerusalem (11.12–13.37)

Passover is both a weeklong festival and a special day of celebration. It memorializes and celebrates the release of Israel from their slavery in Egypt and is the first of three annual feasts on Israel's religious calendar. It is followed fifty days later by Pentecost, a harvest festival, and in the seventh month the combined feast of Tabernacles and Atonement (Lev. 23.1-44). During the days leading up to the Passover Day celebration, Jesus teaches daily on the Temple Mount.

5.2.1 Jesus Faces Opposition (11.12–11.26)

As Mark tells the story of 'Good News' which is to be found in following Jesus, he reports that at the beginning Jesus experienced widespread public approval (1.21-45). However, this initial public approval was soon followed by a variety of episodes where his public approval was tainted by disapproval (2.1–3.34). But now, in Jerusalem to celebrate the Passover week, Jesus experiences almost unrelenting opposition (11.12–12.44).

In the first episode, Jesus passes judgment on an unfruitful fig tree (11.12-14; 20-25). The next day Jesus leaves Bethany to return to Jerusalem (11.12) finding himself hungry, he noticed that a distant fig tree as a possible source of fruit. However, when he approached it, he could see that it had no fruit, because it was not the season for figs (11.13). Having found no fruit, he said to the tree, 'May no one ever eat fruit from you again' (11.14a). Mark adds for the benefit of his readership, 'And his disciples heard him say it' (11.14b). Fast forward to the next day. Jesus and his disciples pass by the same way again, and 'they saw the fig tree withered from the roots' (11.20). Remembering the episode from the previous day, Peter blurted out, 'Rabbi, look! The fig tree you cursed has withered!' (11.21). This episode has not been about a capricious cursing of a fig tree. Rather, Jesus has deliberately used this as an object lesson. This is obvious from Mark's two interjections: 1. and his disciples heard him say it (as they were meant to), and 2. 'look, the fig tree you cursed withered' (as they were meant to see it). This episode has within it a variety of lessons: 1. appearances can be deceiving; 2. ultimately all fruitlessness will come under God's judgment; and 3.

the spoken word, even the most incidental, can exercise great power (11.22-25).

In the second episode Jesus cleanses the Temple. Mark's readers need to know that adjacent to the Temple stalls were set up for use by money changers and merchants. Initially, this was done for the pilgrims who may have had to travel long distances to go to Jerusalem. Note the 'table of nations' present at the Temple on the Day of Pentecost (Acts 2.9-11), but by Jesus' day, what was originally a legitimate service provided to pilgrims had become a place of 'merchandizing', and it is this merchandizing that Jesus interrupts.

On arriving at the Temple, Jesus who came to the Temple prepared to act; he 'began to drive out those who were buying and selling there' (11.15). Specifically, 'he overturned the tables of the money changers and benches of those selling doves' (11.15b). Also, '[he] would not allow anyone to carry merchandise through the temple courts' (11.16). His actions and their justification are prophetic.

He asks,

Is it not written:
'My house will be called
A house of prayer for all nations?'
But you have made it a den of robbers (Isa. 56.7; Jer. 7.11).

Anyone who reads Mark's report about Jesus' actions at the Temple can readily imagine the consternation and chaos that Jesus caused. Also, no one could possibly be surprised about how the day ends: 'The chief priests and the teachers of the law heard this and began looking for a way to kill him' (11.18a). But they could not 'because the whole crowd was amazed at his teaching' (11.18b). Laconically, Mark writes, 'when evening came, they went out of the city' (11.19).

5.2.2 Traps, Tests, and a Conundrum (11.27–12.37)
When Jesus began his ministry in Galilee his initial popularity (1.21-45) was soon overshadowed by growing opposition. Mark records that this opposition consisted of four hostile questions, which he silenced by asking his interrogators a conundrum (2.1–3.6). Now, in Jerusalem to celebrate the Passover, Jesus faces a second set of four tests and traps. Jesus will silence these hostile interrogators with a conundrum of his own (11.27–12.37). These two groups of ques-

tions form an inclusio, showing that from first to last, Jesus ministers under the shadow of the cross.

5.2.2.1 The Chief Priests Question Jesus Authority (11.27-33)

The first attempt to trap Jesus comes from some chief priests,
scribes, and elders. Alert Bible readers will remember that Jesus earlier told his disciples that this is the group that would kill him (8.31;
10.33). They question Jesus, asking him, 'By what authority are you
doing these things?' (11.28). 'And who gave you authority to do
this?' (11.28). Certainly by this point in his ministry, Jesus is too experienced to be trapped by a question like this. Jesus responds with
a counter question. He challenges them: 'Answer me, and I will tell
you by what authority I am doing these things' (11.29). His question
to them is about John the Baptist. He asks, 'John's baptism – was it
from heaven [i.e. God] or from men? Tell me!' (11.29). The chief
priests and their cohorts are caught in a dilemma. To acknowledge a
divine origin will expose their unbelief. On the other hand, to
acknowledge a human origin will antagonize the common people,
for they believe that John was a prophet (11.31, 32). So they give 'a
lame duck' answer; 'We don't know' (11.33). This answer to Jesus'
question silences these enemies and, no doubt, delighted the large
crowd that was gathering on the Temple Mount that day (12.37).

5.2.2.2 Jesus Tells the Parable of the Tenants (12.1-12)

Jesus has just refused to reveal to the chief priests the source of his
authority (11.33). Instead, he tells a parable, which in effect is his
answer. It is a simple yet damming story (12.1-9). The parable is
about an absentee landlord, who prepares a vineyard to be rented
out to tenants. In due time, he sends a succession of servants to
these tenants to collect the rent that is due to him. The first servant
is sent away empty handed (12.3); the next servant is beaten and
sent away with injuries (12.4); the landlord sent another servant,
whom the tenants killed (12.5). Finally, the landlord sent his own
son, whom he loved (12.5). The tenants 'took him and killed him,
and threw him out of the vineyard' (12.6). Jesus asks, 'What will the
owner of the vineyard do?' (12.9a). This is a rhetorical question, as
Jesus' own answer makes plain: 'He will come and kill those tenants,
and give the vineyard to others' (12.9b). This parable fulfills the
Passover psalm (Ps. 118.22, 23):

The stone which the builders rejected
Has become the capstone;
The Lord has done this,
And it is marvelous in our eyes.

Mark reports, 'the chief priests, the teachers of the law, and the elders "got it" – they knew that he had spoken the parable against them' (12.10), but they were afraid of the crowd, that is, 'they were afraid of his influence over the people' (12.12).

Some of Mark's readership in later generations may find the parable to be a bit obscure because they live in a different age and culture. The following perspectives may, therefore, be helpful. The landlord is God, the vineyard is the nation of Israel, and the tenants are Israel's leaders. The servants are the rejected prophets; the most recent of whom is John the Baptist and the landlord's only son is Jesus (Mk 1.11), whom Israel's leadership will soon kill. The landlord will kill the leaders and give the vineyard to others; that is, the Church. This parable has its immediate fulfillment in the death of Jesus this Passover season (8.31; 9.31; 10.32-34). It has a further historical fulfillment in the destruction of Jerusalem in 70 CE, signifying the transition of God's people from Israel to the Church.

5.2.2.3 The Pharisees Question Jesus About Paying Taxes (12.13-17)

The coalition of chief priests, teachers of the law, and elders – who are unable to trap Jesus but with stiffened hatred of him (12.12) – 'sent some Pharisees and Herodians to Jesus to catch him in his word' (12.13). These Pharisees and Herodians may include some of the ones who had plotted to kill Jesus because he had healed a lame man on the Sabbath (3.6). Thus, Mark's readership knows that their apparent respect of Jesus as a teacher is hypocritical. They feign high regard, saying, 'Teacher, we know you are a man of integrity … [and] teach the way of God in accordance with the truth' (12.14). They have carefully and cleverly sprung their trap, thinking that they will catch him on the horns of dilemma. Will they trap him when the chief priests have failed (11.27-33)?

Trying to catch him in his words, they ask him, 'Is it right to pay taxes to Caesar or not? Should we pay, or shouldn't we?' (12.15). As an aside for the benefit of his readership, Mark reports, 'But Jesus knew their hypocrisy' (12.15a). He exposes their hypocrisy, 'Why are you trying to trap me?', he asked (12.15b). 'Bring me a denarius and let me look at it' (12.15). Taking the coin that was handed to him, Jesus asked a rhetorical question, 'Whose portrait is this? And whose inscription?' (12.16). 'Caesar's', they replied. Then Jesus said to them, 'Give to Caesar what is Caesar's and give to God what is God's' (12.17). That's it; no commentary necessary. Mark's conclusion says it all – 'And they were amazed at him' (12.17).

There is at least one take away lesson for Jesus' followers. Give back to government what citizens are duty bound to pay (the coin with its image). On the other hand, give to God yourself (made in his image). Caesar's image and inscription united the state with religion; Jesus' reply separated the state from religion.

5.2.2.4 The Sadducees Question Jesus About the Resurrection (12.18-27)

Jesus has silenced his critics, first the chief priests and then the Pharisees to their own amazement (12.17). Next, the Sadducees will try to trap Jesus. Mark gives his readership the key to the question that the Sadducees ask: 'The Sadducees … say there is no resurrection' (12.18). Their rejection of the resurrection is based on their doctrine of Scripture. They accept only the Law (i.e. Genesis to Deuteronomy) as Scripture. There is nothing in the Law about the resurrection. So therefore, the Sadducees rejected the doctrine of the resurrection, which was so prominent in Pharisaic theology (for example, Acts 23.6-10).

Their question arises out of the practice of levirate marriage (Deut. 25.5-10). This is the practice that if the husband dies without a male heir, his next closest brother was to marry the woman and raise up a son – who is legally the son of the dead husband. An Old Testament example of this is found in the book of Ruth (Ruth 4.1-13). The Sadducees ask Jesus a theoretical question about a woman who, in turn, married seven brothers, but none of these marriages produced a male heir. So, their question was, 'At the resurrection whose wife will she be. Since the seven were married to her?' (12.23). Their question is obviously hypocritical since, as we have already read, 'the Sadducees say there is no resurrection' (12.18).

Jesus' answer is a devasting critique of Saducean theology. He replied, '… you do not know the scriptures or the power of God' (Mk 12.24). Thus, the state of the resurrection body is different from the physical body; it is spiritual – like the angels' (12.25). Further, the Law, itself, teaches the resurrection, for God says, 'I am the God of Abraham'. In other words, God is the God of Abraham, who now lives. Therefore, the Law teaches the reality of the resurrection.

5.2.2.5 A Teacher of the Law Questions Jesus (12.28-34)

Mark reports next that one of the teachers of the Law 'heard them debating' (12.28a). Impressed by Jesus' answers, he asked him, 'of all the commandments, which is the most important?' (12.28b). This young teacher is the first sincere interrogator, in contrast to the chief priests, the Pharisees, and the Sadducees. Jesus answers him accordingly: by first affirming that the most important commandment is the 'shema'. 'Shema' is Israel's confession of faith: 'O Israel, the Lord is one. Love the Lord your God with all your heart and with all your soul and with all your mind and with all your strength' (Deut. 6.4, 5). In fact, as devout Jews, both the teachers of the Law and Jesus began this day by confessing, 'The Lord is one …', but there is also another part to the commandment. In addition to loving God with their entire being, they were commanded to love their neighbors as themselves (Lev. 19.18).[21] Because the young teacher has been sincere and not hypocritical, he approves of Jesus' answer: 'Well-said teacher, you are right in saying that God is one and there is no other but him' (12.32). Not only does the teacher of the Law approve Jesus, but also Jesus approves of him. Mark reports, 'When he [Jesus] saw that the man had answered wisely he said to him, "You are not far from the Kingdom of God"' (12.34).

Note that the law is based on love. It is not about merely keeping the law or outward conformity to a code. Rather, it is motivated and founded upon love. Having observed the skill with which Jesus answered his antagonists, no one dared ask him any further questions (12.34).

5.2.2.6 Jesus Poses a Conundrum (12.35-38)

Mark has just concluded his report about the four questions with the observation that no one dared to ask him any further questions (12.34b). Having silenced his opponents by his replies, he now si-

---

[21] Emil Schürer, *A History of the Jewish People in the Time of Jesus Christ*, II, pp. 456-61.

lences them by posing a conundrum of his own. In Jesus' day, Psalm 110 was widely believed to be a messianic psalm. It is this psalm and this interpretation that forms the basis of his question. He asks, 'How is it that the teachers of the law say that the Christ is the son of David' (12.35). David, speaking by the Holy Spirit (2 Sam. 23.2), said,

> The Lord [Yahweh] said to my Lord [*adonai*]
> Sit at my right hand
> Until I put your enemies
> Under your feet (12.36).

Jesus asks, '[since] David himself calls him Lord, how then can he be his son?' (12.37a). A large crowd has gathered around Jesus and his antagonists and 'listened to *him* with delight' (12.37). Mark could also have added that the *crowd* listened to the deafening sound of silence of Jesus' enemies with delight, for the whole crowd was on his side (10.18; 12.12).

5.2.2.7 Jesus Warns About the Teachers of the Law (12.38-40)

In addition to silencing his critics Jesus also warns the Passover crowd against them. For example, he taught, 'Watch out for the teachers of the law' (12.38). There are two reasons for this warning. First, they perform religious duties for show. For example, 'they like to walk around in flowing robes ... and [they love] the places of honor at banquets' (12.39). Second, they oppress the helpless, such as widows, whose houses they devour. Despite Jesus' warning there are countless people who act like these ancient leaders within Judaism.

5.2.2.8 Jesus Commends a Widow (12.41-44)

The setting of this episode is the 'Treasury' on the Temple Mount (12.41). At one unidentified point during the Passover week, Jesus sat down 'opposite the place where the offerings were put and watched the crowd putting their money into the temple treasury' (12.41a). To no one's surprise, 'many rich people put in large amounts' (12.41b). At the same time, 'a poor widow [also] came and put in two very small copper coins' (12.42). The contrast between 'the large amounts' given by the rich, and the 'two small copper coins' given by the poor widow is an object lesson about values in the Kingdom of God.

Jesus calls his disciples to him to teach them an important lesson. This is the lesson, 'this poor woman has put more into the treasury than all the others' (12.43). Jesus explains that the rich 'gave out of their wealth' (12.44a); in contrast, the woman put in everything – 'all she had to live on' (12.44). The lesson is clear, God values the gift by what is left over – the wealthy still had their riches left over, but the widow had nothing left over – she gave everything she had. This is an easily forgotten lesson in middle and upper class societies.

5.2.3 The Eschatological Discourse (13.1-37)

Mark reports that Jesus began his ministry by teaching 'the time has come. The Kingdom of God is near' (Mk 1.15). Now he is about to tell his readers that the end of the beginning is near. This is the subject of Mark 13. It is identified by various titles. Jesus gives his teaching to his disciples on the Mt. of Olives, opposite the Temple Mount, and it is often called, 'The Olivet Discourse'. However, the subject of Jesus' teaching is the last things (Greek *eschatos*, ἔσχατος), and many Bible readers identify this teaching to be 'The Eschatological Discourse'.

In the decades leading up to the appearance of John the Baptist and Jesus, two of the sects of Judaism had strong messianic and/or eschatological (end times) interests. This interest is found both within the Pharisaic and the Qumranian communities. Qumranian 'End Times' eschatology is the most complex of the two sects. In part, this is because they believe that three messiahs would appear, namely, the prophet and the messiahs of Aaron (i.e. high priests) and Israel (i.e. King). The so-called 'War Scroll' is an expression of the Qumran Covenanters. Rejecting Qumran messianic eschatology with its three messiahs, the Pharisees developed a one-messiah eschatology. This focused on a David-like, royal messiah. One of the Psalms of Solomon expresses this *hope*:

> Behold, O Lord, and raise up unto their King, the son of David,
>> At the time in which thou seest, O God,
>> that he may reign over Israel thy servant
> And gird him with strength,
>> that he may shatter unrighteous rulers,
> And that he may purge Jerusalem from nations
>> that trample [her] down to destruction

> Wisely, righteously he shall thrust out sinners
> from (the) inheritance.[22]

Christian eschatology represents a third option. It differs from
Qumranian eschatology in that it has one messiah and not three;
and it differs from Pharisaic eschatology in that its messiah is a suffering messiah and not a military conqueror.

5.2.3.1 The Disciples Question Jesus (13.1-4)

Jesus' teaching about the end times arises out of one disciple's ex-
pressed admiration of the Temple. As Jesus and his companions are
leaving the Temple, one of them exclaims, 'Look, Teacher! What
massive stones! What magnificent buildings!' (13.1). Even a modern
tourist, seeing the same sight would be equally impressed. The first
century Jewish historian, Josephus, reported, 'Some of the stones in
the building were forty-five cubits in length, five in height, and six
in breath'.[23] In modern measurements, a single stone of this size
would be 67 ft x 7.5 ft x 9 ft. Access to the courtyard was through
any one of nine gates, which 'were completely overlaid with gold
and silver … each gate had two doors, and each door was thirty cubits in height and fifteen cubits in breath' [i.e. 45 ft high and 22.5 ft
wide].[24] Jesus, however, has a different perspective. Jesus replied,
'Do you see all these great buildings? Not one stone here will be left
on another, everyone will be thrown down' (13.1). Any tourist who
might visit Jerusalem today can verify for him/herself the total
completeness of the destruction of the Temple Mount. Jesus and
his companions now leave the Temple Mount, cross the Kidron
Valley, and sit on the Mount of Olives opposite the Temple. Mark
reports that Peter, James, and John privately asked Jesus two questions. Their first question was, '*When will these things happen?*' and the
second was, '*What will be the sign that they are all about to be fulfilled?*'
(13.4). In the so-called 'Olivet Discourse', which follows, Jesus answers both the 'when' and the 'what' questions (13.5-37).

---

[22] Psalm of Solomon 17.23-27 in R.H. Charles (ed.), *The Apocrypha and Pseude-
pigrapha of the Old Testament in English, with Introductions and Critical and Explanatory
Notes to the Several Books* (2 vols.; Oxford: Clarendon Press, 1963), II, p. 667.
[23] Josephus, *Wars*, 5.222-24.
[24] Josephus, *Wars*, 5.210-12.

5.2.3.2 Jesus Teaches His Disciples (13.5-37)

Jesus first answers the question, 'When will these things happen?' (13.5-23). Then, he answers the question, 'What will be the sign that they are all about to be fulfilled?' (13.24). Finally, he concludes his lesson with a stern and strong exhortation, 'Watch, therefore' (13.28-37).

5.2.3.2.1 Jesus Teaches About When the Temple will be Destroyed (13.5-23)
Jesus begins his lesson as he concluded it, 'Watch out that no one deceives you' (13.5). This warning is to alert his disciples that 'many will come in my name, claiming, I am he' (13.6). In other words, end-time prophecy is susceptible to the rise of many false Christ's. Theses pretenders are not only false Christ's, but they deceive others. One test of these false teachers is that in spite of their teaching, and/or predictions, history must run its course. So, for example, 'wars and rumors of wars' do not presage the end times. Wars and rumors of wars are not to alarm the disciples. Indeed, 'such things must happen' (13.7). As history runs its course, there will be international warfare, global earthquakes, and famines. These do not signal the end times, rather than being end times events; *these are the beginning* of birth pangs (13.7).

Because of the presence of the false teachers and their message of deception, the disciples must be on their guard (13.9). In fact, prophetic preoccupation is a distraction. Jesus' disciples are to be busy serving the Lord, but there will be a price to pay: flogging (2 Cor. 11.8), arrest, and trials (13.9b). Nevertheless, they must preach the gospel in every nation (Acts 2. 4, etc.). But the disciples are not abandoned, for the Holy Spirit will speak through them (13.11). For example, Peter and John were filled with the Holy Spirit when they were on trial before the Sanhedrin (Acts 4.8). Similarly, when the synagogue of the Freedmen opposed Stephen, 'they could not stand against Stephen ... or the Spirit by which he spoke' (Acts 6.10). However, this will be an age of unprecedented genocide: 'Brother will betray brother to death' (13.12). Also, fathers will betray his children, and the children will rebel against their parents. Nevertheless, those who stand firm in the faith will be saved (13.13).

Associated with this persecution (13.11-13), the Temple will be destroyed. A time will come when 'the abomination that causes desolation' will stand where it will not belong. The term, 'abomination that causes desolation' comes from the book of Daniel (see Dan. 9.27; 11.31; 12.11). Both in Daniel and in Mark, it describes the practice of emperor worship by the Romans. When the abomination happens, God's people in Judea will flee to the mountains (13.14). This abomination is to be fled instantly (13.15, 16). The destruction will be dreadful – unequaled in the past (such as when Babylon captured Jerusalem [2 Kings 24, 25]) – and never will be equaled again. However, for the sake of preserving God's chosen/elect people, he will shorten the days of dreadful destruction.

Jesus now gives his disciples a further warning about false messiahs (13.21-23). Jesus' message is plain and direct: 'If anyone says to you, "Look, here is the Christ!" or "Look, there he is!" do not believe it' (13.21). The disciples need to be on their guard, because 'false Christs and false prophets will appear' (13.22a). What makes them so dangerous to the unwary disciples is that they will perform signs and miracles to deceive the elect – 'if that were possible' (13.22b). Jesus has now done his part, specifically, 'I have told you everything ahead of time' (13.23). Therefore, now it is up to the disciples to do their part, 'so', Jesus tells them, 'be on your guard' (13.23b). But it is a sad lesson of history, both then and now, that some of God's people are caught off guard.

5.2.3.2.2 Jesus Teaches His Disciples About the Parousia (13.24-27)
The coming of the Son of Man is described in the language of the Old Testament prophets. Referring to the time of distress and false messiahs:

> The sun will be darkened,
> And the moon will not give its light;
> The stars will fall from the sky,
> And the heavenly bodies will be shaken (Isa. 13.10; 34.4).

How different this prophetic language differs from the creation account.

> And God said, let there be lights in the expanse of the sky to separate the day from the night, ... and let them serve as signs to mark the seasons ... God made two great lights – the greater light to govern the day and the lesser light to govern the night.

He also made the stars … And God saw it was good (Gen. 1.14-17).

On those days when God created the heavens and the earth; the creation of the sun, the moon, and the stars contributed to the orderliness of the cosmos and the world. But when Jesus comes at the end of the age, neither, sun, moon, or stars contribute to chaos. And so, the Son of Man of the Gospel will come at the end of the ages to re-order the cosmos so it can function according to its creative and redemptive purposes. In this way, the Son of Man will come in the clouds with great power and glory … and he will gather his elect from the ends of the earth to the ends of the heavens (13.27).

Jesus has in some detail answered the questions posed to him by Peter, John, and James: 'When will these things be?' He has also answered the question about the signs when all these things are going to be fulfilled.

5.2.3.2.3 Jesus Teaches His Disciples To Be On Alert (13.28-37)
The disciples are to learn the lesson of the fig tree (13.28-31). When its twigs get tender and its leaves come out it is evident that summer is near. Similarly, when the disciples see various signs come to pass (13.5-23), they will know that the Coming of Jesus is near, right at the door. Jesus insists, 'I tell you the truth, this generation will certainly not pass away until these things have happened' (13.30). This is a difficult saying for many readers to understand because, in context, there are three possible meanings. The key to sorting them out is to remember that Jesus' teaching answers the two questions posed by the disciples: 1. when will these things happen? 2. What will be the sign that they are about to be fulfilled? (13.4).

If the term 'generations' means Jesus' contemporary disciples, then 'these things' refer to the destruction of the Temple in 70 CE. (13.2). If the term 'generation' means 'race', then 'these things' refer to the woes of history (13.5-23). If the term 'generation' means the generation of the Parousia (i.e. Second coming of Jesus), then 'these things' refer to the cosmic signs (13.24-27).

From the first coming of Jesus to his second coming, history has three stages, and Jesus' multiplex answer has meaning for God's people during each stage in which they are living.

In the light of the fact that some of Jesus' own disciples will live to see the destruction of the Temple, they and every subsequent generation of Jesus' followers are to take heed (13.33-37). Thus, Jesus' disciples and subsequent generations of disciples need to understand that ignorance of the date is no excuse for being unprepared (13.33). Jesus illustrates the need to be prepared from the example of the servants. They are to be on alert for the return of their master (13.34-36). 'So be on guard'. 'Be on guard!' 'Be alert!' 'Therefore, keep watch'. 'What I say to you, I say to everyone: Watch!' (Mk 13.23, 33, 35, 37).

5.3 The Authorities Put Jesus to Death (14.1–15.47)

Jesus' eschatological discourse (13.1-37) ends in a flurry of exhortations and warnings; 'Take heed, watch out, beware'. There is great danger ahead for the disciples, whether they are companions of Jesus or whether they live in more modern times. However, as important as the eschatological discourse is for the disciples, they are in the middle of an ominous crisis – the chief priests, teachers of the law, and the elders are as determined as ever to kill Jesus (14.1, 2). The Passover day is just two days away, and their strategy is to arrest him before the Passover and kill him afterwards. In this way, they hope to avoid a riot against themselves. At this point, Mark has concluded Jesus' public ministry in the Temple courtyards and for the remainder of his narrative focuses on the events related to his death – the first of these episodes is the anointing of Jesus.

5.3.1 A Woman Anoints Jesus (14.3-11)
The anointing of Jesus takes place in Bethany in the home of a man, Simon the leper. Mark does not say so, but he gives the impression that Simon is a hitherto unnamed disciple. Suddenly, 'a woman who is carrying an alabaster jar of very expensive perfume' enters the house (14.3a). To everyone's surprise, and the consternation of some of Simon's guests, she breaks open the jar and pours its contents over Jesus' head (14.3b). Jesus' companions are indignant at the woman's action, for they say among themselves, 'why this waste of perfume? It could have been sold for more than a year's wages and the money given to the poor' (14.4, 5). In their indignation, 'they rebuke her harshly' (14.5b). But immediately, Jesus

comes to her defense insisting, 'she has done a beautiful thing to me' (14.6). 'She did what she could' (14.8). She has poured this perfume 'on my body beforehand to prepare me for my burial' (14.8). Jesus adds an observation; 'you have the poor with you always and have not shown any concern for them'. This exposes their hypocrisy, for they are more interested in her money, than they are interested in the poor. Her care for Jesus will be told in memory of her as long as the Gospel is preached throughout the world.

The episode in which this woman anoints Jesus is an enacted parable, which points to Jesus' death and burial (14.8). For Judas, it also may have been the proverbial 'last straw' or 'the straw that broke the camel's back'. And so, one unintended consequence of the woman's actions is to spur Judas to the most heinous act in human history. He left the home of Simon the Leper in Bethany, 'went to the chief of priests to betray Jesus to them' (14.10). Not unexpectedly, they were delighted by this, and promised to give him money' (14.11).

5.3.2 Jesus Initiates the New Covenant (14.12-31)

Several events come together for Jesus to transform the Jewish Passover to the making of the New Covenant. These include the preparations of eating the Passover supper, a further prediction of Jesus' death, the institution of the Lord's Supper, and Jesus' announcement of Peter's denial.

5.3.2.1 Jesus Commissions Some Disciples to Prepare the Passover Meal (14.12-16)

The first day of the Feast of Unleavened Bread and the celebration of the Passover coincide (14.12). With the help of residents from Jerusalem, Passover pilgrims would prepare the Passover meal. It is in relation to this that Jesus' disciples ask him, 'Where do you want us to go and make preparations for you to eat the Passover?' (14.12). Jesus sends the disciples to go and make the preparations, having already worked out the place – a large upper room – where they celebrate the Passover (14.14). This room is probably the 'Upper Room' made famous in its relationship to the Day of Pentecost (Acts 1.13, 14). The disciples make their rendezvous with the householder, 'and prepare the Passover' (14.16).

5.3.2.2 Jesus Again Announces His Death (14.17-21)

The Passover had great significance, dating back to the Exodus of Israel out of Egypt (Exodus 12–14). It was the beginning of the redemption of Israel from their Egyptian slave masters, their escape from Pharaoh's army, and flight into the Wilderness. At earlier Passover celebrations, Jesus may have celebrated the death of the Passover lamb, but on this Passover day, he is preoccupied with his own death. This evening while he is reclining at the table with his disciples, the Twelve, he said, 'I tell you the truth, one of you will betray me – one who is eating with me' (14.17). Mark reports that his disciples were saddened with this announcement (14.18). Now, the disciples are not saddened by the announcement that he will be killed because he has already told them this (8.31; 9.31; 10.33), but surely the fact that he is about to be *betrayed* should evoke a response stronger than this! This betrayal fulfills a prophecy about the Son of Man. The identity of this traitor is also a matter of prophecy – 'the one who dips his bread in the bowl with Jesus' (14.20). Such a traitor is fully deserving of the 'woe' which Jesus pronounces over him (14.21).

The eating of the Passover meal is a long and drawn out process. At the 'eating of the bitters, Jesus took bread, gave thanks and broke it'. Giving it to the disciples, he said, 'Take it, this is my body' (14.22). This is an obvious echo of the prophetic, miraculous feeding of the five thousand. On that earlier occasion, Jesus took the loaves of bread, gave thanks, and broke the loaves ... until the disciples picked up twelve baskets full of bread left over (6.42-44). The twelve loaves symbolize the whole nation of Israel, just as the twelve disciples symbolize the whole nation. The 'cup of blessing' followed the eating of the bitters. Therefore, 'he took the cup, gave thanks and offered it to them' (including the one who will betray him). They all drank from it! He explained, 'this is the blood of the covenant, which is poured out for many' (14.24). Note that it is poured out for many – that is for the many who will accept him as their Messiah-Christ (14.24). Jesus concludes the Passover meal with the solemn affirmation, 'I will not drink again of the fruit of the vine until that day when I drink it anew in the Kingdom of God' (14.25). Now that the Passover meal has concluded, they sang a hymn. This hymn is Psalm 118, which has appeared before in Mark's narrative (12.10, 11):

The stone which the builders rejected has become the capstone;
The Lord has done this, and it is marvelous in our eyes.
This is the day the Lord has made.
Let us rejoice and be glad in it' (Ps. 118.22-24).

And so, he left Jerusalem with his companions as a lamb led 'to the slaughter' (Isa. 53.7; Rom. 8.36).

5.3.2.3 Jesus Predicts Peter's Denial (14.22-31)

The setting for this episode is the Mount of Olives. 'You will all fall away' Jesus told them (14.27). This falling away is according to prophecy, specifically, 'I will strike the Shepherd, and the sheep will be scattered' (Zech. 13.7), but he also gives them a word of encouragement: 'after I have risen, I will go ahead of you into Galilee' (Mk 14.28). True to his somewhat bombastic character, Peter insists, 'Even if all fall away, I will not' (14.29). As happened earlier, when Peter rebuked Jesus because he talked about a suffering, martyred Messiah, Jesus once again must put Peter in his place. Jesus solemnly insists, 'today – yes tonight – before the rooster crows twice you yourself will disown me three times' (14.30). Clearly, Peter hasn't learned his earlier lesson, and emphatically insists, 'even if I have to die with you I will never disown you' (14.31). Strangely, Peter was telling the truth. He probably was willing to die for Jesus (note that he has equipped himself with a sword, 14.47), but he missed the point. Jesus wanted his loyalty not his heroic, but futile, death. And, following Peter's lead, the other disciples also affirmed that they would not fall away (14.31b).

5.3.3 Jesus is Arrested and Put on Trial (14.32–15.15)

The narrative now moves from the Mount of Olives to the Kidron Valley, which separates the Temple from the Mount of Olives. Here, Jesus has come to pray. His disciples have come with him, but they will sleep while Jesus prays!

5.3.3.1 Jesus Prays in Gethsemane (14.32-42)

It is likely that every time Jesus came to Jerusalem from Galilee, he had come to this olive grove to pray. Incidentally, some of the olive trees in this garden are over 2,000 years old, and still stand as silent witnesses to this scene. Jesus takes Peter, James, and John with him as he goes apart from the other disciples to pray. In his humanity, 'he began to feel distressed and troubled' (14.33). He confessed to his companions, 'my soul is overwhelmed with sorrow' (14.34a). He asks them to stay where they were and to keep watch (14.34b). In the dark night of his soul's distress, he pours out his soul to God, asking that if possible the hour might pass from him (14.36). 'Abba, Father', he prayed (14.36), 'everything is possible for you. Take this cup from me. Yet not what I will, but what you will' (14.36). Visitors to Jerusalem today (not only the curious, but also the devout) can visit the 'Church of All Nations', which is built over the spot where Jesus prayed this prayer of submission to the will of his Abba, Father.

Once! Twice! Thrice! Jesus returned to his disciples to find them sleeping. Even though the apostles are with him, in the end he faces his father alone. Finally, Jesus is at peace. He therefore said to them, 'Enough! The hour has come. Look, the Son of Man is betrayed into the hands of sinners' (14.41). This is an awful irony. In Daniel's vision about the Son of Man, the Ancient of Days gave him, 'authority, glory, and sovereign power ... his Kingdom will be an everlasting Kingdom' (Dan. 7.14, 27), but first he must be betrayed into the hands of sinners.

5.3.3.2 Jesus is Arrested (14.43-52)

The background to Jesus' betrayal and arrest is given by Mark earlier on in this chapter. After Jesus has commended and defended the woman who had anointed him for his burial (14.3-9), Judas Iscariot went to the chief priests to betray Jesus to them (14.10). Now, after his prayer time in the garden of Gethsemane and as he was speaking to his disciples, Judas appeared (14.43). He is not alone. With him is a crowd with swords and clubs. The crowd comes with the authority of the chief of priests, teachers of the law, and elders (see 8.31; 9.31; 10.32-34; 11.27; 12.12, etc.). Going to Jesus, Judas greeted him, 'Rabbi', and by a previous arrangement betrayed him with a kiss (14.44). The crowd seized and arrested him, and at the same time one of his disciples pulls out his sword to defend him. Bible readers generally identify this disciple to be Peter. Jesus submits to his arrest, but rebukes them for not arresting him in the Temple Courts in daylight (something they were afraid to do, 11.18; 12.12). Then everyone deserted him and fled – so much for the assurance to Jesus that they would not all fall away (14.31). Providing comic relief to the scene there was a young man following Jesus. When the crowd attempted to arrest him, he slipped out of their grasp and escaped them, leaving his linen garment behind him (14.52). Could this young man be John Mark, the son of Mary (Acts 12.12), and the author of Mark's Gospel, a generation later?

5.3.3.3 The Jewish Authorities Try Jesus (14.53-65)

The crowd who have arrested Jesus now take him to the High Priest and the coalition of chief of priests, teachers of the law, and elders came together (14.53). Peter's flight is not totally discreditable. Though he fled when the crowd arrested Jesus, he has followed it at a distance – right into the High Priest's courtyard (14.54). He even mustered up the courage to sit with the guards, warming himself by the fire (14.54). As he is warming himself, a servant girl passes by and recognizes him, 'You also were with the Nazarene', she said (14.66, 67). Peter denied it and moved himself away from the fire (14.68). This creates a threefold recognition-denial motif (14.66-69). While he is denying Jesus for the third time, the rooster crows twice (14.66-72). There is nothing that Peter can do – all his braggadocio lies shattered at his feet: 'And he broke down and wept'.

Meanwhile, as Peter is undergoing his baptism of fire in the courtyard of the High Priest, a mock trial – a charade – is taking place inside. The chief priests and the whole Sanhedrin (the governing council within Judaism) were looking for evidence against Jesus. 'However, they could not find any' (14.53). Therefore, they were reduced to concocting some evidence:

> Many testified falsely. Even when some witnesses reported his announcement that in three days he would destroy and rebuild the Temple, their testimony did not agree.

To the aggravation of the High Priest, Jesus would not defend himself. Again, the High Priest asked him, 'Are you the Christ, the Son of the Blessed One?' (14.61). Jesus answered, 'I am'. In fact, 'you will see the Son of Man sitting at the right hand of the Blessed One and coming on the clouds of heaven (14.62; compare Dan. 7.13; Rev. 1.7). The High Priest rent his clothes – Jesus' self-identification is sufficient. He has committed *blasphemy*. This accusation forms an inclusio with the charge of *blasphemy* spoken by some teachers of the law near the beginning of Jesus' ministry (2.7).

Thus, from first to last, Jesus' ministry has been carried out under the shadow of death.

Having found him guilty of blasphemy, all restraining influences are off.

> They spit at him.
> They blindfolded him, struck him, and demanded that he identify his tormenters by a word of prophecy.
> The guards took him and beat him.

And he hasn't even yet appeared before the Roman Authorities!

5.3.3.4 Jesus is Tried Before Pilate (15.1-15)

The trial of Jesus, because of the lack of credible witnesses against him, looks as though it may end in stalemate. However, Jesus bails out the High Priest, by claiming to be 'the Son of the Blessed One', that is 'the Son of Man.' (Mk 14.61, 62). This admission enables the Sanhedrin to find him guilty of blasphemy. However, though the Sanhedrin is the highest court or council within Judaism, its authority does not extend to carrying out executions (Jn 18.23). Therefore, they must go to Pilate, who will have come up to Jerusalem from Caesarea Maritima to keep the peace, not only to ratify their decision but also to authorize the death penalty (Jn 18.31).

As a commentator of Mark's Gospel, I have earlier commented on Mark's style of writing. He often uses an extreme economy of words. In this narrative, he simply reports that the whole Sanhedrin, consisting of the chief of priests, with the elders, and teachers of the law, reached a decision (15.1). Notice that Mark makes no mention of the Pharisees in his description of the Sanhedrin. This might be very deliberate, for the Pharisees made up half of the members of the Sanhedrin. Might this be Mark's way of absolving the Pharisees of Jesus' death? (compare 15.1 with 8.31; 9.31; 10.33; *et al.*). 'Very early in the morning', this coalition of Jewish leaders bound Jesus and brought him to Pilate (15.1b), but Mark does not tell his readership anything more about him. Pilate obviously has more authority than the Sanhedrin, but Mark doesn't identify him as the Roman Procurator or tell his readers that Pilate's official residence is Caesarea, or that there is sometimes friction between the two leading authorities – Roman and Jewish. Furthermore, the Sanhedrin and Pilate, or their representatives, must have had some previous discussion about Jesus, for the first of Pilate's words to Jesus, 'are you the King of the Jews?' (15.2).

'Are you the King of the Jews?', Pilate asked Jesus. To Pilate this is a political question and is an important question to the one who is responsible for governing a people who are already predisposed to rebel against Roman authority (Mk 14.48; 15.7). Without discussion or defense, Jesus simply declares, 'Yes, it is as you say' (15.2b). Thus, Jesus accepts the accusation, but of course, it has spiritual meaning for him (compare 1.15), and the discussion about Kingship between Pilate and Jesus has an ambivalence of differing connotations (political vs. spiritual). The chief priests and Pilate continue to press Jesus for an unambivalent answer, 'but Jesus still made no reply' (15.5). Pilate was amazed because, from his perspective, he controlled Jesus' fate.

The chief priests and the coalition, which they represent, have not been able to present a compelling case against Jesus, and Pilate is not interested in having Jesus executed. So, there is somewhat of a deadlock between the two authorities. Pilate does possess some good political skills and he offers the Sanhedrin an option. As a gesture of good will the Roman authorities would release a prisoner at Passover time (15.6). This Passover one of the candidates for release was a certain insurrectionist by the name of Barabbas. In modern terminology, he would be known as a political terrorist. The crowd ask Pilate if he was going to release a prisoner this year, as he had done in the past (15.8). Pilate gives the Jews an option. Apparently, he seems to think that they will choose Jesus, the King of Jews, rather than Barabbas, a murderer. In other circumstances, the crowd may have chosen Jesus, but this Passover, 'the chief of priests stirred up the crowd to have Pilate release Barabbas instead' (15.11).

So, Pilate is left to deal with the chief priests, who are envious of Jesus. The magnitude of their envy is evident in the fact that they prefer a murderer, rather than Jesus, who has committed no crime (15.9, 14). The magnitude of their envy and hatred is also evident in the fact that they want Jesus to be *crucified* (15.13, 14). Crucifixion in New Testament times was *normally limited to slaves*. In this way Pilate has backed himself into a corner. He is to treat an innocent man as if he were guilty of a crime, as if he were a slave rather than a free man. Therefore, wanting to pacify the crowd, he releases Barabbas, and then has the Roman soldiers flog Jesus, adding injury to insult (15.16).

5.3.4 The Roman Soldiers Mock Jesus (15.16-20)

Jesus' trial before the Sanhedrin ended with Jesus being ill-treated by some of its members (15.16). Similarly, his trial before Pilate ended in ill treatment by the Roman soldiers. After Barabbas has been released Jesus was flogged, with as many as 39 lashes being applied. In addition to the brutal flogging, for example, they dressed him in a purple robe, the color that most symbolizes royalty (15.17). They also plaited a crown of thorns with which they crowned him. As if this mockery is not enough, they called out, 'Hail, King of the Jews!' (15.18). Neither were they content with having flogged him, but, repeatedly, 'they struck him over the head with a staff' (15.19). They mocked him further by falling on their knees before him. Having satisfied their lust for cruelty, they strip him of his purple robe and dress him again in his, by now, blood stained robe.

5.3.5 The Soldiers Crucify Jesus (15.21-32)

Having made sport of Jesus, the Roman soldiers now lead him out of the Palace (i.e. Praetorium) to crucify him. Jesus has just experienced savagely brutal treatment twice within the last twelve hours. It seems that it is impossible for him to carry his own cross. And such is the case. So, they forced a certain Simon from Cyrene in North Africa. Possibly, but not certainly, he was one of the Passover pilgrims who filled Jerusalem. Also, likely, but not certainly, he was to carry only the crosspiece. He picks up his cross to follow Jesus – and somehow became a believer. Mark's readership knows this, because he has met Simon's son, Rufus, in Rome (Rom. 16.14). Jesus will be crucified at the place called 'Golgotha', which means 'Place of the Skull' (15.22). This place seems to be the place outside of Jerusalem where crucifixions regularly took place. For several generations, Protestant Christians have claimed that the skull-like rock formation in modern Jerusalem is Golgotha. It is often identified as 'Gordon's Calvary' after the nineteenth century British explorer and adventurer Charles Gordon. But, careful archeological exploration in Old Jerusalem indicates that this identification is almost certainly wrong. Having brought Jesus to the Place of the Skull, they offered Jesus a sedative, which was a mixture of wine and myrrh (15.23).

Jesus refuses to take it (15.23), and after this, 'they crucified him' (15.24). Mark's readership may presume that Jesus was 'nailed' to the cross, which is confirmed by the wounds in his hands (i.e. his wrists). Next, the soldiers cast lots to see who would get his clothes (15.24).

Mark reports that Jesus was crucified at the third hour (15.25). This is the time when the daily morning sacrifice was being made at the Temple, a short distance away. Many of Jesus followers noticed the coincidence at the timing and its significance for the meaning of Jesus (compare Rom. 3.21-25). The written notice of the charge against him 'identified him as the King of the Jews' (15.26). Jesus was not the only one who that day was crucified in Jerusalem (15.27). Two robbers, that is, two insurrectionists, were also cruci- fied – 'one on the right and the other on the left' (15.28). Death by crucifixion was often a lengthy process, and as Jesus hung on the cross, some passersby hurled insults at him (15.29). Jesus' claim to rebuild the Temple in three days after its demolition seems to have been a common subject of mockery. So, he is taunted, 'come down from the cross and save yourself' (15.30).

Not only did those passing by mock Jesus, but so did the chief priests and the teachers of the law (15.31). 'He saved others', they said among themselves, 'but he can't save himself' (15.31). In fact, they challenged him, 'Let this Christ, this King of Israel come down now from the cross' (15.32). They promised that if he would come down, 'they will see and believe' (15.32b). This mockery echoes that of the Pharisees, who after Jesus has multiplied food to feed the crowd of four thousand (8.1-10), ask Jesus for a 'sign from heaven' (8.11). Jesus refused to perform miracles from heaven then (8.11- 13), as he refuses to do miracles now. Jesus knows that miracles *may* make believers out of believers, but, typically, they do not make be- lievers out of unbelievers. Even those who were crucified with him 'heaped insults on him' (15.32c).

5.3.6 Jesus Dies (15.33-41)

Jesus endures the suffering of hanging on the cross from the third hour to the sixth hour (i.e. 9.00 a.m. until noon, 15.33). Jesus has ignored the taunts and insults from the different groups who make up the crowd of spectators. Now, at the noon hour, the brightest time of the day, God blots out the light of the sun until the ninth hour (15.33b). This is Jesus' 'dark night of the soul' and at the ninth hour he cries out to God in a loud voice, '*Eloi, Eloi, lama sab-bachthani*' (15.34b). In this time of desolation, he feels that all that he has left are the scriptures, such as Ps. 22.1, which he has just begun to pray. This abandonment is to be understood in the light of the fact that 'God made him who had no sin to be sin for us, so that in him we might become the righteousness of God' (2 Cor. 5.21; compare also Gal. 3.13, 14). One commentator on the Gospel wrote, 'It is in the cry of dereliction that the full horror of man's sin stands revealed'.[25] The cry, '*Eloi, Eloi*' was misunderstood to be the cry for the similar sounding of the prophet Elijah. In later legends, Elijah was considered by Jews to be a helper in time of need.[26] Jesus, who was hung on the cross for six hours, was offered some wine, which he refused. Another spectator said, 'Leave him alone. Let's see if Elijah comes to take him down' (15.36). However, at this time 'with a loud cry, Jesus breathed his last' (15.37). When he cried out, 'the curtain of the Temple was torn in two from top to bottom' (15.38). This veil separated the holy place from the holy of holies. The tearing of the veil has declared that Jesus had opened the way into the presence of God. This veil is described in the Mishnah:

> The veil was one handbreadth thick and was woven on a loom having seventy-two rods, and over each rod were twenty-four threads. Its length was forty cubits and its width was twenty cubits; it was made by eighty-two young girls, and they used to make two in every year; and three hundred priests immersed it (*Shekalim* 8.5).

A Roman centurion, captain of one hundred soldiers, witnessed the way Jesus died and was transformed. He exclaimed, 'Surely this man was the Son of God!' (15.39). Some scholars interpret what he said to mean that Jesus was 'a demi-god, a hero'. However, in Mark's Gospel, the term in context does mean 'Son of God' in the Christian sense of the phrase. The following texts illustrate this:

Mark 1.1: Mark introduced Jesus as the Christ, the Son of God.

Mark 1.11: The voice from heaven declared, 'You are my Son'.

---

[25] Cranfield, *Mark*, p. 458.

[26] Cranfield, *Mark*, p. 459.

Mark 9.7: The voice from heaven declared, 'This is my Son, whom I love'.

Mark 15.39: The centurion exclaimed, 'Surely this man was the Son of God.

This declaration of the centurion is the climax of Mark's Gospel. It is also the climax of Mark's four portraits of Jesus: 1. teacher (1.21–4.45), 2. prophet to Israel and the Gentiles (5.1–7.37), 3. Messiah (8.1–9.50), and finally, 4. King of the Jews (10.1–15.47). Therefore, Jesus' Kingship is unique, for it is the kingship of the Son of God. It is also the answer to Jesus' conundrum, explaining how David's son is David's Lord (Mk 12.35-37).

Public executions, particularly the executions of 'notorious' persons, often attract a crowd of spectators. These may be the hostile or caring. Such is the case with the crucifixion of Jesus. Not all of the spectators were hostile. There was a small group of (mostly) women watching the crucifixion from a distance (Mk 15.40). This group of women was 'the last at the Cross, and the first at the tomb'. The watchers included Mary Magdalene, Mary the Mother of Jesus, with her two sons, James and Joseph (compare 6.3), and Salome, Mary's sister. Mark reports that in Galilee these women, and others, 'had followed him and cared for his needs (15.41). Many other women, Passover pilgrims from Galilee were also there.

5.3.7 Jesus is Buried (15.42-47)

Mark reminds his readership that Jesus was crucified on Preparation Day (that is, the Day before the Sabbath, 15.42). At this point, Mark introduces into his narrative a certain prominent member of the Sanhedrin, Joseph of Arimathea. He was a devout man, 'waiting for the Kingdom of God'. Mark reports that as the evening approached he 'went boldly to Pilate, and asked for Jesus' body' (15.43). Pilate was surprised that Jesus had died so quickly, and asked for a centurion to verify that Jesus was indeed dead (15.45). Once this was done, Pilate gave the body to Joseph (15.45). Joseph made the necessary preparations for Jesus' burial. He bought some linen cloth, took down the body, wrapped it in the linen, and placed it in a tomb cut out of rock (15.46). Finally, he rolled a stone against the entrance of the tomb (15.47a). These are the details of a traditional burial – the rock cut tomb, the linen, the body bound in linen, etc. All of these details show that he had no expectation that Jesus would rise from the dead. On this matter, Joseph is like the apostles, who refuse to believe the reports of Jesus' resurrection (Mk 16.11, 14, *et al.*). While Joseph of Arimathea has been preparing Jesus' body for burial, Mary Magdalene and Mary the mother of Jesus' brothers[27] observed where he was laid.

---

[27] Mark is reluctant to identify Mary as Jesus' mother. He identified her as the mother of James and of Joseph (15.40, 47). This is to cover her identity and to protect her from Jewish or Roman hostility.

MARK 16.1-20

EPILOGUE

Epilogue: He Has Risen (16.1-20)

6.1 The Resurrection of Jesus (16.1-8)

On the day before the Sabbath, Joseph of Arimathea made prelimi-
nary preparations for the burial of Jesus' body (15.42-47). At this
time, in Jewish burial practice, a body was given a temporary burial,
and once it was reduced to skeleton, the bones were put in a stone
box, which normally had an inscription that identified the person
who had been buried. The box was the then placed in the niche of
the wall for permanent burial. Mark reports that after the Sabbath
was over, the women who had been last at the cross came first to
Joseph's tomb to make initial preparations for Jesus' burial.

Jesus, his disciples, his family, and other companions had come
to Jerusalem to celebrate Passover. Naturally, they did not bring
along with them the materials that were necessary for a burial.
These now had to be purchased, therefore, 'after the Sabbath was
over, Mary Magdalene, Mary the mother of James and Salome
bought spices so that they might go to anoint Jesus' body' (16.1).
Next, very early on the first day of the week, 'just after sunrise, they
went on their way to the tomb' (16.2). The phrase, 'just after sunrise', indicates that they were on their way about six o'clock in the
morning, but they had to deal with one big problem. 'Who will roll
the stone way from the entrance of the tomb?' (16.2). When they
looked up, they saw that the stone had been rolled away. Entering
the tomb, they saw a young man dressed in a white robe. Bible
readers typically identify this person to be an angel, but Mark does
not. Seeing the young man sitting on the right side, they were
alarmed (16.5).

The young man allays their fear, saying, 'Don't be afraid' (16.6).
In fact, he has good news for them. This good news is that Jesus
the Nazarene 'has arisen! He is not here' (16.6). As proof of the

resurrection, 'the man directs the ladies to see the [empty] place where they laid him' (16.6b). The ladies are to be messengers to the resurrection – a surprise since at the time women were not allowed to be witnesses at a trial, but the ladies are to 'go, tell the disciples and Peter' (16.7). 'They will meet him again in Galilee' (16.7). The women, trembling and bewildered, fled from the tomb. The news that Jesus has so often suppressed – namely, that he is the Messiah – can now be broadcast throughout Galilee – but the women were too afraid to tell anyone! (16.8).

THE END. ALMOST!

The NIV Translation of Mark's Gospel ends with the following statement:

> The earliest manuscripts and some other ancient witnesses do not have Mk 16.9-20.

Whether or not Mark wrote these verses, they have the quality of 'self-authentication' and will be commented upon in this commentary. These verses fall into three paragraphs: 1. Jesus appears to various followers, 2. Jesus recommissions his disciples, and finally, 3. Jesus ascends in heaven.

6.2 Jesus Appears to Various Disciples (16.9-14)

Mark or some anonymous author reports, 'early on the first day of the week, he [Jesus] appeared first to Mary Magdalene' (16.9). This is the Mary 'out of whom he had driven seven demons'. She is one of the women who were last at the cross and first at the tomb (see 15.47, 16.1). After Jesus had appeared to her, 'she went and told those who had been with him' (16.10). When they heard that 'she had seen him, *they did not believe it*' (16.11). Similarly, Jesus appeared to two disciples (16.11), but he was in a different form (i.e. his resurrected body, 16.12). When these two disciples reported their experience 'to the rest, *they did not believe them either*' (16.13). Finally, Jesus appeared to the Eleven as they were eating (16.14). A principle in Jewish law is that 'A matter must be established by the testimony of two or three witnesses' (Deut. 19.15), but the disciples do not believe the two witnesses. Therefore, when Jesus appeared to the

Eleven, he rebuked them 'for their lack of faith and their stubborn refusal to believe' (16.14).

6.3 Jesus Recommissions His Disciples (16.15-18)

Early in his ministry, Jesus commissioned the twelve disciples 'that they might be with him and he might send them out to preach and to have authority to drive out demons' (3.14, 15). Now, after the resurrection, Jesus recommissions his disciples, who have recently been disloyal, traitors, disbelieving, and hard-hearted. He commissions them to 'go into all the world and preach the gospel' (16.15). Note that Mk 1.1 – the beginning of the Gospel of Jesus Christ – indirectly reports the record of Peter's preaching in Rome. Earlier, Jesus' public ministry is to preach the gospel (1.14) in Galilee (1.1–9.50). The disciples are heirs to Jesus' ministry but are to preach to all the creation (16.15). Jesus' preaching of the gospel required the response of faith (1.15). Similarly, the disciples' proclamation of the gospel also stands in contrast to the unbelief of the disciples to the resurrection reports (16.11, 13). To preach the gospel is not only a matter of prophetic words, but also, as in Jesus' own ministry, it is also a matter of prophetic works. These works are, of course, miracles, both for Jesus and also for the disciples. And, by the gifts of power and authority, they are of the same kind. Therefore, as they go out to proclaim the good news they will also demonstrate the gospel by casting out demons and healing the sick (16.17-18).

6.4 Jesus Ascends into Heaven (16.19, 20)

After Jesus has recommissioned his disciples, he ascends into heaven. That is, he ascended into God's presence (16.19). Again, with the outmost economy of words, Mark now records the fact of his enthronement, 'He sat at the right hand of God'. He had submitted to God's will in the garden of Gethsemane (14.36), and now it is fitting for God to enthrone him as his co-regent. Similarly, the disciples now begin to minister according to their recommissioning, 'and the Lord was with them and confirmed his word by the signs that accompanied it' (16.20).

MAP OF PALESTINE IN THE TIME OF JESUS

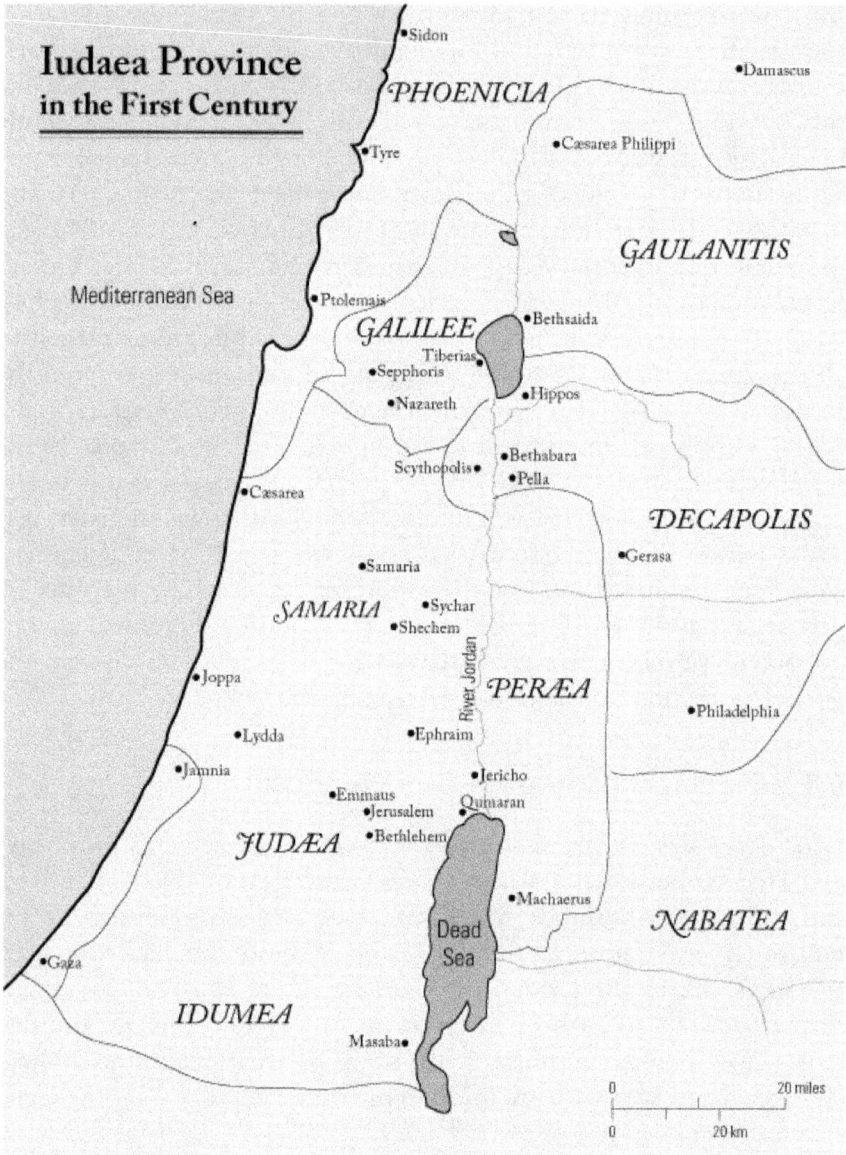

Iudaea Province
in the First Century

• Sidon

PHOENICIA
• Damascus

• Tyre
• Cæsarea Philippi

Mediterranean Sea
• Ptolemais
GAULANITIS

GALILEE
• Bethsaida
Tiberias
• Sepphoris
• Nazareth
• Hippos

• Bethabara
Scythopolis •
• Pella
• Cæsarea
DECAPOLIS
• Gerasa

• Samaria
SAMARIA
• Sychar
• Shechem

River Jordan
PERÆA
• Philadelphia
• Joppa
• Lydda
• Ephraim
• Jamnia
• Jericho
• Emmaus
• Jerusalem
Qumaran
JUDÆA
• Bethlehem

• Machaerus
NABATEA
Dead
Sea
• Gaza
IDUMEA
Masaba •

0   20 miles

0   20 km

SELECTED BIBLIOGRAPHY

General

Bruce, F.F., *New Testament History* (Garden City: Doubleday, 1969).

Ferguson, Everett, *Backgrounds of Early Christianity* (Grand Rapids: Eerdmans, 1987).

Jeremias, J., *Jerusalem in the Time of Jesus* (London: SCM Press, 1969).

—*New Testament Theology* (London: SCM Press, 1971).

Moore, G.F., *Judaism in the First Centuries* (New York: Schocken, repr, 1971).

Schurer, Emil., *History of the Jewish People* (Vols. 1-3; Edinburgh: T&T Clark, 1973).

Stevens, William H., *The New Testament World in Pictures* (Nashville: Broadman, 1987).

Tenney, Merrill, *New Testament Times* (Grand Rapids: Eerdmans, 1965).

Commentary Series

The Anchor Bible
Ancient Christian Commentary on Scripture
Baker Exegetical Commentary on the New Testament
The Communicator's Commentary
Cornerstone Biblical Commentary
The Daily Study Bible
The Expositor's Bible Commentary
Harper's New Testament Commentaries
New American Commentary
New Century Bible Commentary
New International Biblical Commentary
New International Commentary on the New Testament
New Testament Commentary
The New Testament Library
NIV Application Commentary
The Pillar New Testament Commentary
Tyndale New Testament Commentaries
Word Biblical Commentary

Dictionaries

Collins, John J., *The Eerdmans Dictionary of Early Judaism* (Grand Rapids: Eerdmans, 2010).

Evans, Craig A. and Stanley E. Porter (eds.), *Dictionary of New Testament Backgrounds* (Downers Grove: InterVarsity Press Academia, 2000).

Green, Joel B., Scot McKnight, and I. Howard Marshall (eds.), *Dictionary of Jesus and the Gospels* (Downers Grove: InterVarsity Press, 1992).

Green, Joel B., *Dictionary of Jesus and the Gospels* (Downers Grove: InterVarsity Press, 2013).

Martin, Ralph P. and Peter H. David (eds.), *Dictionary of the Later New Testament and Its Development* (Downers Grove: InterVarsity Press, 1997).

Special Studies

Arrington, French and Roger Stronstad (eds.), *Life in the Spirit New Testament Commentary* (Tulsa, OK: Empowered Life Academic, 1999).

Bartholomew, Craig, Joel B. Green, and Anthony Thistleton (eds.), *Reading Luke: Interpretation, Reflection, Formation* (Grand Rapids: Zondervan, 2005).

Beasley-Murray, G.R., *Jesus and the Kingdom of God* (Grand Rapids: Eerdmans, 1986).

Blomberg, Craig, *Jesus and the Gospels* (Nashville: Broadman and Holman, 1997).

Bock, Darrell L., *A Theology of Luke and Acts* (Grand Rapids: Zondervan, 2012).

Burge, Gary, *Interpreting the Gospel of John* (Grand Rapids: Baker, 1992).

Bystrom, Raymond, *God Among Us: Luminaire Studies* (Winnipeg: Kindred Publishers, 2003).

Carrol, John T. and Joel B. Green, *The Death of Jesus in Early Christianity* (Peabody: Hendrickson, 1995).

Collins, John J., *The Scepter and the Star* (New York: Doubleday, 1995).

Currie, Robin and Stephen Hyslop, *The Letter and the Scroll* (Washington, DC: National Geographic, 2009).

Drane, J., *Jesus and the Four Gospels* (San Francisco: Harper & Row, 1979).

Evans, Craig A. and James A. Sanders, *Luke and Scripture* (Philadelphia: Fortress, 1993).

France, R.T., *I Came to Set Fire on the Earth* (Downers Grove: InterVarsity, 1975).

Garland, David E. *A Theology of Mark's Gospel* (Grand Rapids: Zondervan, 2015).

Green, Joel B. and Michael C. McKeever, *Luke-Acts and New Testament Historiography* (Grand Rapids: Baker, 1994).

Green, Joel B. and Lee Martin MacDonald (eds.), *The World of the New Testament* (Grand Rapids: Baker, 2013).

Guthrie, Donald, *Jesus the Messiah* (Grand Rapids: Zondervan, 1972).

Hooker, Morna D., *The Signs of a Prophet* (Trinity Press International, 1997).

Isbouts, Jean-Pierre, *The Biblical World: An Illustrated Atlas* (Washington, D.C., 2007).

Jenkins, Philip, *Hidden Gospels* (New York: Oxford University Press, 2001).

Johnson, Luke Timothy, *The Gospel of Luke* (Collegeville, MN: Liturgical Press, 1991).

–*Prophetic Jesus, Prophetic Church* (Grand Rapids: Eerdmans, 2011).

Keener, Craig S., *The Bible Background Commentary* (Downers Grove: InterVarsity, 1993).

Koester, Helmut, *Ancient Christian Gospels: Their History and Development* (Philadelphia: Trinity Press International, 1990).

Lawrence, Paul, *The IVP Atlas of Bible History* (Downers Grove: InterVarsity, 2006).

Letham, Robert, *The Work of Christ* (Downers Grove: InterVarsity, 1993).

Longenecker, Richard, *The Christology of Early Jewish Christianity* (Naperville: Allenson, 1970).

Lucado, Max, *Just Like Jesus* (Nashville: Thomas Nelson, 1998, 2008).

MacLeod, Donald, *The Person of Christ* (Downers Grove: InterVarsity, 1998).

Marshall, I.H., *I Believe in the Historical Jesus* (Grand Rapids: Eerdmans, 1977).

–*The Origin of New Testament Christology* (Downers Grove: InterVarsity, 1976).

McKnight, Scot, *Interpreting the Synoptic Gospels* (Grand Rapids: Baker, 1988).

Morris, Leon, *The Apostolic Preaching of the Cross* (Grand Rapids: Eerdmans, 1955).

Parsons, Mikeal C., *Luke: Storyteller, Interpreter, Evangelist* (Peabody: Hendrickson, 2007).

Stein, Robert H., *The Method and Message of Jesus' Teaching* (Philadelphia: Westminster, 1975).

–*The Synoptic Problem: An Introduction* (Grand Rapids: Baker, 1987).

Stott, John R.W., *The Cross of Christ* (Downers Grover: InterVarsity, 1986).

Strobel, Lee, *The Case for Christ* (Grand Rapids: Zondervan, 1998).

Stronstad, Roger, *The Charismatic Theology of St. Luke* (Peabody: Hendrickson, 1984).

—*A Pentecostal Biblical Theology: Turning Points in the Story of Redemption* (Cleveland, TN: CPT Press, 2016).

Wenham, David and Steve Walton, *Exploring the New Testament: A Guide to the Gospels and Acts* (Downers Grove: Intervarsity, 2001).

Wright, N.T., *Jesus and the Victory of God* (Philadelphia: Fortress Press, 1997).

INDEX OF BIBLICAL AND OTHER ANCIENT REFERENCES

AUTHOR INDEX

www.ingramcontent.com/pod-product-compliance
Lightning Source LLC
Chambersburg PA
CBHW072350090426
42741CB00012B/2991